D1605937

Global Jumpstart

Other books by Ruth Stanat

The Intelligent Corporation
Global Gold

Other books by Chris West

Marketing Research
Marketing on a Small Budget
Inflation—A Management Guide to Survival

GLOBAL JUMPSTART

The Complete Resource for Expanding Small and Midsize Businesses

Ruth Stanat and Chris West

PERSEUS BOOKS
Reading, Massachusetts

Copyright © 1999 by Ruth Stanat and Chris West

Perseus Books is a member of the Perseus Books Group.

Jacket design by Peter Blaiwas
Text design by Joyce C. Weston
Set in 10.5-point Sabon by Carlisle Communications

Library of Congress Card Catalog Number: 98-88635
ISBN 0-7382-0020-4

123456789-DOH-0302010099
First printing, November 1998

Perseus Books are available at special discounts for bulk purchases in the U.S. by corporations, institutions, and other organizations. For more information, please contact the Special Markets Department at HarperCollins Publishers, 10 East 53rd Street, New York, NY 10022, or call 1-212-207-7528.

Find us on the World Wide Web at
http://www.aw.com/gb/

To my three children, Scott, Christine, and Michael, and especially to my husband, Bill—without his support, the book would not have been possible.

— Ruth Stanat

To my wife, Frances.

— Chris West

Contents

Preface

We are very excited to have the opportunity to write this book specifically for small to midsize firms as they face the challenges of participating in this exciting and dynamic global marketplace. During the past two to three decades of our careers and businesses, we have assisted larger firms throughout the world in their global business-expansion efforts. Now the time has come for smaller firms to participate in these opportunities.

Global Jumpstart represents our combined experience of monitoring the successes and failures of many companies throughout the world. The next millennium will open the door for a new wave of global pioneers in their search for global profits. To aid in this process, we have developed this complete resource guide for small to midsize firms. *Global Jumpstart* is a primer, which enables smaller firms to develop a global mind-set, to determine whether they are candidates for global expansion, and to learn how to research global markets to utilize their limited resources effectively and to minimize their risks in these markets.

Global Jumpstart is rich in case studies of firms that have capitalized on the global marketplace. It also distills the overwhelming task of global research, selling, exporting, and marketing into a simple guide for the smallest of companies. *Global Jumpstart* enables firms to take not only a larger view of the world, but also a different view of themselves and of their future into the next century. Through writing *Global Jumpstart,* we are able to offer our expertise, thinking, and guidance. We would like to thank Ms. Tiffani Wroblewski for her hard work and dedication to the development of the book.

Introduction

As the world turns global, few businesses can ignore the global marketplace. In particular, small to midsize firms face the challenge of determining whether their businesses are candidates for global expansion and, if so, how to get started. The thought of going global may seem overwhelming to chief executives or management teams, who may therefore seek external support. *Global Jumpstart* is a complete resource guide for small to midsize firms that are contemplating expanding their businesses globally. It is also designed for firms who may have already expanded their businesses into other countries or regions of the world, either successfully or unsuccessfully, as well as those who sense that they need to participate in the global marketplace if their business is to survive into the next century.

Global Jumpstart is a first step in the process of changing a company's future. Small to midsize firms have limited resources in comparison to large, multinational firms. Yet there are numerous opportunities for smaller firms to target their products and services, to select countries and regions, and to reap the benefits of the dynamic global marketplace. *Global Jumpstart* provides a framework to help business executives navigate this complex and overwhelming process. As a complete resource guide it will help minimize the risk of failure inherent in global marketing through a step-by-step approach to research and analysis of global business opportunities. *Global Jumpstart* will enable executives to develop a plan for the globalization and organization of their firms and will provide resources to execute the plan.

Chapter 1 discusses the global business marketplace and includes numerous examples of small businesses that have successfully created market niches in select global markets. The chapter also outlines the forces that contribute to the continued development of global business as well as global pitfalls. Chapter 2 addresses the issue of determining whether

---

The contributing author to this section was Craig Palubiak, president, The Optim Consulting Group, St. Louis, Mo.

a business is a candidate for global expansion. It explains how to decide if the firm has the financial or human resources to execute a global program and what changes need to be made in an organization to support a global program.

Chapters 3 through 5 contain the rudiments and specifics of research and planning for the globalization process. These chapters provide a rigorous overview of the principles and tools necessary for global research, intelligence, and information gathering. Chapter 3 outlines a methodology for conducting a global marketing audit, which is essential to focusing the analytical effort. Chapter 4 details a specific analytical process for evaluating global opportunities. Chapter 5 outlines the various types of research that are available to an organization and provides a process for the development of a strategic opportunity grid. This process enables the business executive to evaluate business opportunities on a global basis, rather than to follow a knee-jerk reaction and rush headlong into the next hot country.

Moving beyond the fundamentals of the research and planning process, Chapter 6 provides a wealth of information on options for going global. This chapter introduces foreign market entry, exporting (through a step-by-step approach), and alternative methods of foreign market entry (e.g., licenses, franchises, and strategic alliances).

Chapter 7 discusses the challenge of global selling and the necessity for knowledge of the local cultural conditions of the country. As the process of going global means changes at home as well, Chapter 8 addresses organizational issues and details a step-by-step approach for a planned and successful international program. Lastly, Chapter 9 explains how to measure success in global markets.

Having secured *Global Jumpstart,* you may be asking, "How do I get started?" One of the first steps is to develop a global mind-set. Global business development starts in the mind of the CEO or head of a small to midsize firm. Once you have made the decision to go global, you can proceed to the next step, the business development process. Business development should be and often is a primary concern of the CEO and should include strategic planning, business research and market intelligence gathering, and business development.

Very simply, business research and market intelligence gathering provide insurance policies against being blindsided when entering foreign markets. Too often, companies enter a foreign market without being fully aware of local customs, conventions, consumer attitudes and preferences, local distribution channels, governmental policies, and, most important, local competitive conditions. Very often, a firm will sign an agreement with a local distributor only to learn eventually that the distributor also represents several other domestic and foreign competitors, and it can be very difficult to terminate distributor relationships in some countries. Even worse, small to midsize firms often underestimate the power of local competitors and their capabilities to develop technology and improve the quality of their products.

Global Jumpstart underscores the need for research, research, and more research. The research chapters in this book provide a wealth of information to enable you to look before you leap and know the lay of the land prior to market entry. Specifically, they will help you conduct the following four essential steps in global business development.

Step 1: Conduct Market Research Within Your Budget

In a world in which knowledge is power, market research is a vital component in the global marketing process. The unknowns in national markets are considerable, but internationally they are multiplied by a huge factor. Without data the chances of making serious errors in both planning and executing global marketing strategies are too high to contemplate. Research is rarely cheap, but companies must be prepared to make some up-front investment to reduce risk. Fortunately, support is often available for small- and medium-size firms in the form of finance, expertise, and other assistance from government agencies with a mission to promote the exploitation of overseas markets. Small- and medium-size global marketers must develop skills to seek out and exploit to the fullest what is available.

 Case Study
Research Helps Write a New Chapter for Communication Intelligence Corporation

Through careful research, Communication Intelligence Corporation (CIC), Redwood Shores, California, was able to capitalize on a market opportunity for its product in China. CIC is a publicly traded company, founded in 1981. Revenues for fiscal year 1995 were $2.3 million; approximately 30 percent came from overseas sales. The company has a wholly owned Japanese subsidiary and a 79 percent interest in a joint venture in the People's Republic of China. One of CIC's products is the Handwriter for Windows, an ultrathin digitizer table bundled with pen-computing software that enables users to enter graphics, text, and computer commands as if they were writing on a pad of paper.

Through market research, CIC determined that the People's Republic of China (PRC) was its next big new market. According to CIC management, "We expect China to be one of the fastest growing markets in the next ten years, and we are developing input devices that will make it easier for the Chinese people to interact with computers in their own language." The Chinese language consists of thousands of complex ideographic symbols, which makes it inherently difficult for keyboard entry. CIC developed handwriting-recognition technology to enable users to enter Chinese text in their own handwriting, without a keyboard. This technology was tested toward the end of 1996, and CIC began selling its products through the PRC joint venture in the second half of 1997.

CIC had received a NIST Advanced Technology Program (ATP) grant from the National Institute of Science & Technology of approximately $1.2 million in 1991, which enabled it to develop a significant part of the technology that went into the Handwriter product and to assemble teams and accelerate R&D to reduce the time to market. In addition, the award increased CIC's credibility, helping the company establish licensing arrangements for its technology. In November 1993, CIC received a second ATP award of $1.5 million, which enabled it to proceed with R&D of the input technology for the PRC market. This second award also enabled CIC to develop an international team, based in the United States, to produce the technology. According to CIC's management, this grant was critical because CIC could not fund the research in a timely fashion on its own. Moreover, delay can kill promising technology or leave it to be taken over by foreign competitors.

Step 2: Assess Your Internal Resources

Any firm, large or small, must have an international general or an international champion who initiates this effort and is the driving force behind its implementation. In small firms (i.e., $1 million to $100 million in revenues) this person is usually the CEO or president. In larger firms

($100 million to $300 million in revenues), this person may be the CEO, president, vice president of sales or marketing or, if the first steps have been taken, vice president of international business development. In most cases, at least 30 to 50 percent of this person's time will be dedicated to expanding the business internationally. Most international firms will want to deal only with the CEO, president, or key decision maker for contract negotiations, strategic alliances, distribution agreements, and so on. *Global Jumpstart* also discusses the need for appropriate technological resources (fax machine, e-mail system, and, preferably, a web site for marketing products) and for the appropriate level of financial resources (e.g., a cushion in case of adverse events, a travel budget, and a budget for expert advice).

 Case Study
Ostrich Rancher Keeps Head Out of Sand, Looks to Feather His Nest in Overseas Markets

Zion View Ostrich Ranch, in St. George, Utah, has experienced great success in the United States as low-fat ostrich meat is being sold in retail and health food stores. The firm is a ten-person, 250-acre operation that raises ostriches for meat and other products. Zion View first entered the domestic marketplace in late 1995, but is just beginning to tap the Japanese and European markets as part of its strategic plan to capitalize on the worldwide increase in health consciousness. The firm has taken advantage of the Commerce Department's trade services (e.g., obtaining market data and taking advantage of counseling and key contacts). Clearly, Zion View needs the dedication of an international champion to further global expansion.

Step 3: Get Yourself Export Ready
Formulating a solid export strategy requires a critical examination of the capabilities and resources of your company as well as consideration of several important questions, such as what countries to target, what strategy to use in addressing import barriers, what the time frame will be and when to phase in activity, and what cost, in both time and money, to expect.

🌐 Case Study
Indiana Cash Drawer Got Itself Export Ready

Indiana Cash Drawer, Shelbyville, Indiana, founded in 1921, is a privately held company that for seventy-five years has manufactured cash drawers in wood and steel. These drawers are used in a variety of applications—manual, electronic interface for electronic point-of-sale systems, and PC based—and in a variety of markets—general retail, hospitality and fine dining, banking, convenience stores, and pharmacies. From 1993, the company started distributing and selling other companies' point-of-sale peripherals. These now constitute about one-third of the company's sales.

For years, Indiana Cash Drawer had a limited number of inquiries from overseas buyers. As competition in the domestic industry grew fierce, it explored other worldwide markets and made a strategic decision to pursue them. At that time, exports accounted for less than 1 percent of the company's revenue. Today, exports account for almost 10 percent of revenue. Indiana Cash Drawer is establishing a worldwide presence. It has recently inaugurated a new plant in Mexico. As a result, it has increased its staff in Indiana from sixty-five to one hundred employees. In two years, the company expects its exports to reach 30 percent of revenues.

Indiana Cash Drawer became export ready through several face-to-face meetings with International Trade Administration (ITA) staff on export markets and on exporting in general. Along with established distributorships in Luxembourg and Croatia, in early 1994 the company utilized the ITA's Gold Key program in Mexico and as a direct result found a distributor in that country. In the first year, sales in Mexico were half a million dollars. By the second year, Indiana Cash Drawer's export sales to Mexico had increased by 33 percent. Later in 1994, the company used the ITA's Gold Key service again in Hong Kong, Singapore, and Taipei. Through these efforts, Indiana Cash Drawer now has a dealer in Hong Kong that buys its products. The most valuable information provided to Indiana Cash Drawer by the ITA was that the firm was further behind in its ability to meet the strong demand of the Asian markets than it had thought. Indiana Cash Drawer has also used ITA's overseas offices to distribute literature and other materials, resulting in additional export sales around the globe. In short, this company became export ready through the assistance of a local ITA office at minimal cost.

Step 4: Adopt a Global Mind-Set

The most important step in taking your company global is adopting or embracing a global mind-set. Your global mind-set is your vision of the future picture of your firm. If you are not absolutely convinced that your firm should expand into global markets and not totally committed to the business-development process, you should reevaluate your strategy. A global mind-set will enable you to weather the changing global (and domestic) business conditions. The highs will be high, but the lows can be extremely low when unexpected events happen in the global marketplace. Most important, your firm is equally, if not more, at risk in your domestic marketplace through increased foreign competition than in foreign markets. Remember, those small firms that adopt a global mind-set will become the midsize firms of the twenty-first century.

> *Many small and midsize companies can't overcome the psychological barriers to international business even when a tremendous opportunity may be within their reach.*

We often hear about the comeback of professional athletes, but rarely do we hear about the comeback of a New England textile company. Quaker Fabrics, which dates back to the 1930s, has passed through several names and owners. It was publicly traded as Vertipile in 1989, when it was purchased and taken private by an investor group led by Larry Liebenow, who is now Quaker's CEO. Liebenow adopted a global mind-set and implemented a two-pronged strategy of modernizing equipment and aggressively pursuing international markets.

In the 1960s and 1970s, Quaker was a significant exporter; then it discontinued these efforts. With the implementation of the North American Free Trade Agreement (NAFTA), Liebenow's international strategy focused primarily on Canada and Mexico. The strategy has paid off. In just a few years, foreign sales have grown to 15 percent of the company's profit and total sales have doubled to $196 million in 1996.

Liebenow notes that many midsize companies can't overcome the psychological barrier to international business, so they leave it to larger, multinational companies, even though a tremendous opportunity may be within their reach. By hiring people who were convinced that Quaker could compete worldwide, the company vanquished those fears. This story is an example of giving customers what they want, when they want it.

Quaker's global mind-set has also enabled it to capitalize on the rising income levels in Asia and Latin America, which are creating strong markets for U.S. furnishings. Although countries such as India, Pakistan, and the People's Republic of China are off limits to U.S. textile producers, Quaker Fabrics is actively seeking other available markets. The global mind-set of this firm has helped restore the reputation of Fall River, Massachusetts, as a premier textile and upholstery source.[1]

 Case Study

Success Story of a Company with a Global Mind-set, Plan, and Strategy

Evan Ballman, age forty-five, is the president of Motor Appliance Corporation (MAC). Founded in 1946, MAC manufactures custom AC induction motors for original equipment manufacturers and industrial battery chargers. Its headquarters is located in St. Louis, Missouri, and it has manufacturing facilities in the Midwest.

A few years ago, Ballman recognized that MAC's marketplace was reaching maturity. Ballman knew it was time to jumpstart his business by expanding outside the United States with an international strategy. He was guided by three critical issues: (1) new growth opportunities would arise with the increased demands of the international marketplace for innovative products to handle such concerns as energy conservation and pollution; (2) MAC's own customers were becoming more involved with the global marketplace as they sought new, high-growth markets; and (3) MAC itself could benefit from lower-cost suppliers based outside the United States.

While searching for new opportunities, Ballman met Chandu Vanjani, who had over thirty years of international experience in the design and manufacturing of electric motors. Vanjani had worked as a project engineer and product manager for major firms in India and the United States. He had also managed his own brushless DC (BLDC) motor manufacturing firm.

In 1996, Ballman and Vanjani joined forces and formed a new venture named MAC BMC. Their goal was to target profitable, international niche-market opportunities for BLDC motors and controls. They realized that the $1 billion BLDC motor market was a fast-growing segment of the $30-billion electric-motor industry for several reasons:

- The BLDC motor is substantially smaller in size and weight than conventional AC or DC motors.
- Variable speed control provides flexibility in optimizing running conditions.
- The BLDC motor requires little or no maintenance because it has no mechanical brushes.
- The BLDC motor is more energy efficient than conventional AC motors and pollutes less than small combustion engines.

The key to MAC BMC's success was the development by Vanjani of a proprietary design that ensures consistent, high-quality motors at very competitive prices. Historically, BLDC motors have not been competitively priced in the markets identified by MAC BMC because of high material and manufacturing costs.

Based on primary and secondary research, MAC BMC identified three different segments of the motor market to target. The first focuses on replacing conventional, battery-powered electric motors in such items as commercial and industrial equipment. The second is the replacement of conventional AC or DC motors in such applications as fans and pumps. The third segment includes applications that currently use small, internal-combustion engines, such as gas-powered bicycles and scooters.

This third segment is of particular interest as individual and world governments begin to mandate a reduction in energy consumption and pollution. Among the applications that appear to offer significant short-term potential are electric-powered two-wheel vehicles. For example, massive air pollution has resulted in Asia as thousands of people have shifted from manual bicycles to gas-powered bicycles. In this case, electric bicycles are seen as a viable solution to reducing not only air pollution but also gas consumption.

Research indicates that there are numerous BLDC motor manufacturers, but MAC BMC considers few of them to be potential competitors in the near term. Many of these firms target markets such as factory automation and computer peripherals, segments that do not interest MAC BMC. Furthermore, BLDC motor companies tend to focus on either the controls (drive electronics) or the motor; MAC BMC has the advantage of doing both well.

Entrants to the BLDC motor market face several obstacles. First, they must have significant capital, knowledge, and technical expertise to manufacture low-cost BLDC motors. Second, they must be accustomed to application development and systems engineering. Third, they must enter the market quickly, before opportunities disappear. And last, international marketing to original equipment manufacturers is a complicated and time-consuming process when a company is trying to establish solid business relationships.

MAC BMC's strategy consists of three primary components: design, manufacturing, and marketing. Design is an ongoing process, influenced by both current and future marketplace needs. MAC BMC is working closely with numerous customers and prospects in developmental alliances. Some of these alliances are with current Motor Appliance Corporation customers who are in MAC BMC's first two target markets. As these applications continue to prove out, MAC BMC expects to develop relationships with many of its international affiliates. This has already begun to occur.

In the electric-vehicle market, developmental alliances have been established both domestically and abroad. Partners include domestic manufacturers that will sell as well as export products in the United States and large foreign manufacturers of vehicles. MAC BMC has strategically targeted these relationships by making contact directly with the top management of the organizations.

MAC BMC is currently manufacturing motors on a limited basis at its new plant in Bombay, India. Recognizing the importance of local support, the owners recruited a Bombay citizen, a business associate of Vanjani, to manage the plant. Local representation adds credibility when dealing with the Indian government and Indian businesspeople. Under proprietary agreements, MAC BMC has also established relationships with other foreign manufacturers in the event that additional capacity is needed for quick jumps in demand.

Marketing is perhaps the biggest challenge faced by MAC BMC. The first two target markets are being developed domestically through Motor Appliance Corporation, which has an established network of clients and prospects. These relationships have resulted in numerous design activities as well as in product purchases. In some situations, the customer's international affiliates have begun to deal with MAC BMC directly. The domestic two-wheel manufacturers are being targeted by

Ballman and Vanjani. One of the manufacturers has invested financially in MAC BMC's design efforts and is now ready to reap the benefits of its investment by delivering large quantities of product through the international distribution channels it has put in place. Ballman and Vanjani have spent substantial time personally marketing their product throughout Asia to the top management of two-wheel manufacturers. Results have been excellent. Several firms are currently in the design stage with MAC BMC. Various types of partnerships have been developed, and joint ventures are in the works. In one case, MAC BMC is working with a government entity and a foreign manufacturer to develop a commercial product jointly. The ultimate goal of MAC BMC is for its international customers to handle the bulk of the marketing, as MAC BMC's motors will be distributed as a component within their finished products.

Ballman and Vanjani feel their opportunities in the international marketplace are limitless. However, they recognize that success depends on their ability to move quickly in delivering a quality, low-cost product. They also recognize that their customers must be more than just customers—they must become partners in their success.

Whether or not you decide to expand your business globally, global business expansion should be a part of your strategic-planning thinking process. As you read *Global Jumpstart,* ask yourself these questions:

- Is my company a candidate for global expansion?
- Do I have the global mind-set to move my firm into the global marketplace?
- Am I willing to commit the time and energy to accomplish this task?
- Am I willing to commit resources to do the homework that is necessary for foreign-market entry? Can I commit the resources to continually monitor these markets?
- Am I willing to assume the risks that are involved in international business development?
- Do I have the patience to remain in select international markets for the long term?

If you can answer yes to each of these questions, then after reading the research methodology and the case studies in this book, you should be able to take action to enter or expand in the dynamic global marketplace. Opportunities will continue to surface throughout the world. Although opportunities may shift among regions of the world, they will not be reduced. Remember, if you don't take advantage of them, someone else—perhaps your local or global competitors—will. The key to success in global markets is *research, timing,* and *patience.* Let *Global Jumpstart* be your guide in this process.

CHAPTER 1

The Global Business

During the 1980s global expansion tended to follow political developments designed to reduce trade barriers and encourage greater movement of people and capital as well as of goods and services. Much of the effort was focused on North America, Europe, and Asia. As the European Union matured and expanded to include most of the smaller European countries, global companies were encouraged to set up plants, offices, and distribution points, safe in the knowledge that they had access to an affluent customer base of over 200 million people. A major part of that encouragement stemmed from the perception that it was better to be inside the camp looking out, rather than outside the camp trying to break in. The demise of communism in Eastern and Central Europe led to a rush of firms seeking to take an early stake in markets that were thought to be bound to expand. The formation of trade pacts, such as the North American Free Trade Agreement (NAFTA) and Mercosur (a trade pact among Brazil, Argentina, Paraguay, and Uruguay), resulted in the acceleration of investment and trade in Latin America. In addition, Asia seemed to become the economic engine of the next millennium, with the rapid growth of the Asian "tiger" economies, along with the Association of Southeast Asian Nations (ASEAN) and China and India. The setback to this position in the late '90s is likely to be temporary.

What opportunities exist for the small to midsize firm in this changing world? The boundaries are changing between countries, between continents, and across cultures. Technology, communications, and transportation have changed the world. Products can arrive across oceans and continents within hours. Information takes seconds to be downloaded, uploaded, and accessed throughout the world. How can you and your business survive and participate in this changing world?

The Global Marketplace

The race for globalization, particularly in the mid-1990s, has produced the concept of a global marketplace, which could be taken to mean that companies need the ability to provide a product anywhere, anytime, to a local market. However, there are four basic approaches to participation in the global marketplace:

1. Exporting your existing products to a foreign market
2. Modifying your products to fit the cultural and environmental requirement of foreign markets
3. Filling a market niche in a foreign market
4. Creating a new and unique market niche in a foreign market

Exporting Your Existing Products to a Foreign Market

Exporting is the most obvious, and usually the least risky, method of gaining a stake in the global market. It also requires the least commitment, which might be advantageous in terms of minimizing the use of resources, but results in a penalty when it comes to the emotional commitment to the development of overseas business. "Easy in" is usually matched by "easy out." Because contact with export customers tends to be more spasmodic than with those in the domestic market, exporters are more than normally influenced by isolated events and impressions. Unless continuous reporting procedures are in place, these may be picked up only when staff travel to overseas markets. Although this can add an element of luck to the export opportunity identification process, it can still have favorable results. In 1989, Steve Marci was eating a $110 lobster at a restaurant in Germany when he realized that someone was making a killing on the clawed creature. Because meatier Maine lobsters live only in North American waters, they sell at exorbitant prices elsewhere. "I saw an opportunity there," he said. "It was the best $110 I ever spent." Now Marci, his wife, and their partner, Roberto Cavallarin, manage S&S Seafood in Northwood, New Hampshire, which has grown from $2 million a year in sales in 1994 to an expected $12+ million in sales by the end of this decade.

Finding the lobsters was easy; the trick was packing them to survive the trip overseas. There was no shortage of buyers. Weekly sales of fifteen thousand pounds of lobster to restaurants in Germany and Italy in the early and mid-1990s ballooned to sixty thousand pounds to twelve countries in Europe and Asia by 1998. Marci's large-scale shipments have brought down the price—now Germans pay about $65 for a lobster dinner—but there is still room for a tidy profit, and that has attracted competition.

Like an old-fashioned business, this business demands personal contact with buyers and a string of small suppliers along the New England coast. Each deal usually requires only two phone calls. If a buyer needs five thousand pounds of lobster in Paris the next day, Marci knows where the supply is and what airline can ship it there. According to Marci, the Internet will not sell lobsters for you and it won't find them for you. Lobsters will die in someone's tank if you don't get them immediately. There is no time for lawyers or contracts![1]

Modifying Your Products to Fit the Culture and Other Demands of Foreign Markets

Sometimes you have to modify your products to fit the cultural and other demands of foreign customers. The Atlanta-based Coca-Cola Company has been successful with this approach. Coca-Cola has produced and sold its traditional soft drink throughout the world, but understands that outside the United States the beverage of choice might not be the "classic" product. International sales in more than 195 countries account for three-fourths of its revenue, and Coca-Cola has developed more than 150 different types of beverages to gratify the tastes of a broad range of foreign consumers.

Soft drinks that are popular in other parts of the world, but are not sold in the United States, run the gamut from mineral water to a mango fruit-pulp concoction. To develop beverages that can compete in foreign markets, the company conducts research, uses phone surveys, and conducts focus groups to analyze tastes. In India, Coca-Cola markets bottled beverages such as Limca (a tangy lemon-lime drink) and Maaza (a noncarbonated mango drink with fruit pulp). To satisfy consumers' tastebuds, it has produced an iced coffee in a variety of flavors—from bitter black to milk-rich café au lait—and Saryusaisai, an iced oolong tea. Of course, Coca-Cola also produces its old standby—plain water.

BonAgua, Coca-Cola's purified mineral water, is a hit in more than thirty-five countries.[2]

Filling a Market Niche in a Foreign Market

A country's political and economic legislation and regulations may dictate that products and services be provided in a certain way (e.g., regulated or provided by the government). If this situation exists for your product domestically, there may be opportunities for you in other countries that have different regulations.

Applied Sweepers Incorporated of Falkirk, Scotland, is sweeping up profits by providing the world with spiffy sidewalks. Founded in 1965, the company expanded a decade later during the era of privatization of government services in the United Kingdom. The current wave of downtown-improvement projects in the United States has opened a booming new market, and the company has found U.S. streets truly paved with gold as a market for its Green Machine. According to Francis Galashan, who directs the U.S. operation from an office outside Philadelphia, Applied Sweepers' twin-brush machines are currently removing litter from New York, Boston, Baltimore, New Orleans, and Philadelphia.

In Europe, governments are responsible for cleaning the sidewalks, but in North America, property owners are responsible for their own territory, and many have joined forces to hire private cleaners. Applied Sweepers opened its U.S. office in March 1998 and has since sold more than sixty machines at $20,000 to $25,000 each. With $30 million in sales last year, the company enjoys about 30 percent annual growth. In 1992, only 10 percent of sales were attributable to exports, compared to 70 percent in 1998.

Two sweeper machines used in New York's Times Square were nicknamed Felix and equipped with a microchip recording of actor Tony Randall warning walkers to "Move it!"—people in the United States are attracted by novelty. The mayor of Baltimore spends about $280,000 for a cleaning that used to cost $1 million. Productivity and convenience have increased while costs have decreased.[3]

Creating a New and Unique Market Niche in a Foreign Market

To succeed in taking a perishable, consumer food product into the international market, a very small U.S. company would need determination, commitment, and much hard work, as well as some good U.S. government connections. With just these elements Diana's California Cookies was able to reach an agreement to have its product made in Ireland and marketed throughout the European Union.

Based in Orange County, California, Diana's California Cookies is the creation and one-person operation of Diana Todero. She developed the recipes for her gourmet, all-natural cookies in her own kitchen, and she contracts with an Orange County bakery to produce them. Todero handles all the sales and marketing herself and has landed accounts at several retail food-store chains and hotel food services in California. Since 1991, Diana's has been very successful in penetrating the California market, selling over one million cookies in the first three months of 1991 and growing ever since. Todero has taken advantage of several of the services offered by the U.S. Commerce Department; she has developed a close rapport with U.S. Export Assistance Center (USEAC) staff in Newport Beach, California, and participated in President Clinton's Conference on Investing in Ireland. These activities have been instrumental in the company's efforts to expand into the European Union, the Middle East, South America, Japan, and other Asian markets.

Todero intended to take her products overseas from the beginning, but she recognized that a one-person firm did not have the resources that larger corporations had and she turned to the U.S. Department of Commerce for help. She was initially interested in exporting her products to Japan and Denmark, but after reviewing market reports provided by the USEAC, she decided that those were not the most suitable markets for the company's first international effort. In her search for more appropriate initial markets, Todero participated in international conferences and events (e.g., the White House Conference on Investment in Ireland). She also participated in two Commerce Department Matchmaker trade missions.

Diana's California Cookies was the first company involved in the White House Conference to achieve a joint-venture marketing agreement in Ireland. Todero credits the conference and the contacts she made with the Irish Food Board during the trade mission for bringing her together with Braycott Foods, the Irish bakery that will produce and sell her cookies in Ireland. Braycott Foods, Limited, located near Dublin, is a sixteen-year-old bakery with twenty-eight employees. Annual sales are in excess of $3 million and expected to climb by 25 percent in 1999. Braycott was looking for an American cookie to sell in the Irish and European markets and believes that Diana's California Cookies has a very strong product

whose health-conscious image and palm tree–sun logo are instantly iden-
tifiable as American.

According to Todero, who is targeting the Middle and Far East and
South America, prospects in these countries look good. Her company is
trademarked internationally, and she is currently reviewing licensing re-
quests so that new business in the European Union and Japan will be
ready to take off without delay. Todero believes that her liaison with the
Commerce Department led to her success.[4]

Forces That Contribute to the Continued Development of Global Business

In 1998 the top 150 CEOs in the United States, collectively known as the
Business Council, met in Washington, D.C., recently to hear President
Clinton extol the virtues of the global marketplace. The largest U.S. companies and their foreign operations now contribute massively to U.S. domestic corporate profits. The question currently facing these business
leaders is, "What will come next?" Many corporate executives credit the
trend to globalization with helping smooth out the up-and-down cycle
of domestic business activities that has interrupted economic expansions
in fairly regular waves in the past.

Many argue that globalization has reduced the threat of the surge of
inflation and rise in credit costs, as in past cycles. According to Jack
Welch, the CEO of General Electric, an analysis of the peak-to-trough
cycles beginning in 1960 shows that they have become more benign with
every decade. As information technology, supply-chain management,
and inventory management have improved on a global basis, the ability
to respond to these cycles has become much faster and more effective.
The peak-to-trough cycle changes of 3 to 4 percent in the '70s have become 1 to 2 percent in the '90s. This is not new, but is supposedly a forty-
year phenomenon.

Alan Bossidy, CEO of Allied Signal Corporation and president of the
Business Council, believes that everyone everywhere wants a job. Thus
the competition is to keep prices down and productivity up. Recessions
are born of excess inventories, excess inflation, excess prices, and excess
wage demands. Although not every global manager is thrilled by this
prospect, these market-stabilization factors will continue to fuel the acceleration of a world marketplace.[5]

Global Pitfalls

You are probably overwhelmed with the thought of going global or exporting your products and services to another country. The companies that have experienced the highest rate of success with their globalization efforts have developed a global mind-set and adopted a "we can do it!" attitude toward international business development. Going global carries the following risks, however:

- Failing financially in foreign markets
- Draining limited domestic human and financial resources
- Ignoring the domestic market
- Giving foreign competitors direct-market and local access to your products and services
- Being unable to obtain financing for exporting your products
- Being unable to locate the right local representative in certain countries

On the other hand, with increased globalization of worldwide product and financial markets, you could face the following risks if you do not consider global expansion opportunities:

- Competitors taking advantage of international expansion opportunities (through exporting their products, strategic alliances, or foreign direct investment)
- Foreign competitors entering your domestic market with improved technology, improved products or services, unique market niches, or better prices
- Losing human resources to firms that are global and offer richer career opportunities
- Experiencing severe swings in domestic business cycles (e.g., recessions)
- Having limited sources of supplies or raw materials for your business

Breaking into the Global Marketplace

Small to midsize firms face less risk than larger (*Fortune 500*) firms. Typically, larger, multinational firms have to make significant capital investment or foreign direct investment (FDI) to compete in the worldwide marketplace. Because these firms have built market-share dominance in their domestic markets, they seek aggressive market expansion in international markets. This globalization effort generally involves a significant investment in the following activities:

- Market research
- Negotiations with country governments regarding legislation and privatization and distribution issues
- Development of a plant, sales facility, or distribution facility
- Expatriates and hiring local personnel
- Local marketing, advertising, and promotion

In comparison, a small to midsize firm can initiate a globalization effort with minimal investment. In the simplest case, a small firm can dedicate the efforts of one person, with a fax machine and computer. You can implement the following minimal-cost strategies for exploring international business opportunities:

- Have your firm's international champion contact the local branch of the International Trade Association for lists of countries that may have need of your firm's products or services.
- Within the United States, purchase information from the Department of Commerce. For as little as $25 per report (e.g., global country reports), these reports provide a comprehensive overview of the country, its economy and political structure, imports, and exports as well as a list of business opportunities.
- Contact local embassies for a list of foreign trade missions, trade fairs, conferences, and seminars in your area and in the local country.
- Make an exploratory trip to the country of interest. With a moderate travel expense, you can make numerous contacts who are potential customers, suppliers, and distributors in that country.
- Low-budget trips to foreign countries can be used to conduct your own market research and market intelligence by checking out the customer base, flow of goods, product prices, consumer traffic flow, local product quality, distribution, and so on. Maximize your travel dollars.
- Obtain cost-effective market research from the Internet and other published sources.

- Market your products globally with a home page on the Internet. Develop a message that leverages the transportability of your products and services.

A small company can project an international image by adding the word *International* at the end of its name. Once the domestic market (domestic customers and competitors) perceives that a firm is international, the firm may be approached by foreign firms for trade opportunities. Although the learning and experience curve in developing and conducting international business is steep, there is no substitute for just doing it. No two countries are the same. Each country has its unique culture, trade regulations, marketplace, distribution channels, legislation, and economic and political structure. The firms that develop the international mind-set, enlist the help of effective organizations, and "just do it" are the firms that win at the global game. The following case study provides an example of a small firm that took this route and has experienced success.

 ## Case Study
Rocket Man Incorporated Gets a Quick Education

The president of Rocket Man Incorporated, LaGrange, Kentucky, describes the company's products as mobile drinking systems. The signature product, the backpack drink dispenser, is used by walking vendors at stadiums to serve hot or cold drinks—beer, soda, hot chocolate. Another major product, the beverage cart with an umbrella, is used at festivals and amusement parks. Rocket Man's products are designed for selling more drinks to more people in more places through mobility.

Rocket Man is a privately held company established in 1992. It has 16 full-time employees and another 150 part-time employees who work at stadiums and special events. Its growth rate was 300 percent between 1993 and 1994 and 225 percent the following year. In the United States, Rocket Man sells to the major beverage dealers, such as Coca-Cola and Miller Brewing Company. Seventy percent of its sales are exports; it ships products to over forty countries. Its overseas strategy is to sell through stocking distributors—people who inventory products to have them on hand for the end users.

Rocket Man first contacted the International Trade Administration in 1993, after receiving a call from a foreign customer. The company knew nothing about exporting and was looking to the Chamber of Commerce for help. The local international trade specialist advised Rocket Man on locating and using government programs and gave the company a start finding distributors in Mexico and Canada. The specialist worked with Rocket Man to refine its export strategy, addressing such issues as setting prices from one country to another, determining what language should be used in a written contract, finding someone who could speak the language, identifying what information was needed from prospective distributors, and evaluating whether the company was dealing with the right prospects. For example, one prospect ready to place an initial order wanted exclusivity in the United Kingdom. Without the specialist's advice, Rocket Man would have agreed to those terms. As it turned out, there were two better long-term prospects who were not in a position to buy right away; Rocket Man signed with one of them.

The ITA specialist consulted with Rocket Man on letters of credit, terminology, what to insure, and so on. Whenever the company came across a new concept, it called on the international trade specialist to be educated. Rocket Man is a prime example of how the ITA can assist companies that have little or no international experience by providing information and education that would take the company years to acquire on its own.

Where Is Global Business Going?

At the start of the next millennium, select regions of the world will fuel or drive the worldwide economy. Asia is expected to be the engine of the twenty-first century. Most of the economies in the Chinese Economic Area (CEA) and the ASEAN countries are expected to experience annual growth rates in excess of 7 to 8 percent over the next five to seven years. Most of these countries (e.g., China, India, Indonesia) are defined as emerging-growth countries, which require investment in their basic infrastructure (transportation, health care, communications, education, etc.). Latin America, with a composite of developing and emerging-growth countries, is the second most promising region for growth. Developing countries (e.g., Chile, Brazil, Argentina) are defined as countries with annual gross domestic product (GDP) rates of 4 to 6 percent having investment in existing infrastructure.

Although Europe and North America are termed mature economies (annual growth rates of 2% to 4%), they will still present export and investment opportunities into the next century. Market segmentation will be critical in these mature economies; they are highly developed and technological leaders, and only niche brands or products are likely to succeed in these markets. Finally, although the Middle East comprises undeveloped consumer and industrial economies, this area will remain less popular because of political uncertainty in the region.

The most important questions you need to consider as they relate to your small to midsize firm are:

- What regions of the world are target areas for your products or services?
- Should you take a global or a country-by-country approach?
- Where do you begin?
- How do you begin?

The following section will lend some insight into how some small firms approach these issues.

Every Company Can Play

There are three critical factors for success in international expansion for small to midsize firms:

1. Develop a global mind-set—either "Do it!" or "Don't do it!"
2. Do your homework.
3. Once you make the commitment, stick with it—develop a long-term plan.

According to Joseph Monti of Grant Thornton Management Consultants in Los Angeles, before manufacturers enact their finely crafted export strategies and other plans to expand into the global marketplace, they need to understand that success in foreign markets rarely occurs by accident. In his company's annual survey of American manufacturers, Monti indicated that a huge distinction exists between understanding the value of global opportunities and knowing just how to launch an international program effectively.

A company considering going international should do its homework on the specific country or countries that it is targeting, rather than on an entire continent or region. Monti holds that it is crucial to build product identity by determining what will sell, what is currently available in the target country, and what competitive advantages the product has. Treat your foreign operation as an integral element of your core business. Visit the countries in which you hope to do business. There's no substitute for a face-to-face meeting, especially in Asia, where relationships drive business dealings.

You should be ready to be as flexible as necessary. What would take a few hours in the United States could take up to three days in some other countries. Monti recommends preparing to make a long-term commitment to the effort and allocating sufficient senior-management time to directing foreign operations. Businesses often underestimate the time required of their senior executives in the United States to keep foreign operations running smoothly. Top executives tend to think that once the deal is done, they can walk away and let the business run itself, that as long as the checks keep coming, their level of involvement can be reduced to a minimum.

Finally, Monti recommends learning the local business practices, finding a local partner, and keeping pace with current developments and worldwide trends. Ignoring trends could, at worst, reduce profitability and, at best, result in international customers rejecting your company's products altogether. International expansion will not lead to quick rewards. Building the right relationships, selecting the appropriate partners, and cultivating a solid client base all take time. It is not, however, time wasted, but time invested.[6]

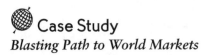 Case Study
Blasting Path to World Markets

The last siren sounds. It's one minute to countdown. Across the way, crowds linger behind television cameras ready to capture the moment for local newscasts. A cloud of smoke and a mountain of dust mushroom through the air as onlookers' jaws drop at the sight before them. For a select few with a close-up view, however, the scene signifies another satisfied client.

Engineered Demolition, Incorporated, is just one of a few companies worldwide that undertake explosive demolition in metropolitan areas. The company's reputation thrives on leaving its customers in the dust.

Engineered Demolition's president, Anna Chong, and her husband, Eric Kelly, are experts in explosive demolition, or implosion, and their Minneapolis-based firm's high and hazardous work is giving clients a real bang for their buck. Implosion destroys a structure by causing it to burst inward, or undergo violent compression. According to Chong, there is an increasing worldwide demand to make more efficient use of costly and limited land space by removing old structures. Her firm's portfolio includes demolition of old commercial buildings, steel mills, nuclear power plants, piers, and smokestacks, among other structures. Although more established in North America, implosion is gaining acceptance in such regions as Asia, Europe, and Latin America, where people have had little previous exposure to explosives or the implosion process. As a result, Chong is taking on quite a bit of consulting work with government agencies and construction firms in their international market.

Canada is Engineered Demolition's largest and most accessible market outside the United States, owing in large part to its proximity and similar culture and way of doing business. Other foreign markets pose a greater challenge. Obtaining a permit is time-consuming in most foreign countries. A country might have permits for rock blasting and tunnel blasting, but no blasting procedures for tall buildings, so they have to be developed. Some countries require a U.S. implosion firm to obtain an in-country license.

There are specific cross-cultural concerns when doing business in the Asian region. As Chong notes, some cultures are superstitious. In Japan and Korea, for instance, the number four means death, so in those countries Engineered Demolition does not demolish structures on the fourth of the month and often avoids loading explosives on the fourth floor of a building. Chong also points out that Asian clients don't always feel comfortable having a woman push down on the detonating device, or plunger, because they believe it may bring bad luck. And Chong keeps a ceremonial plunger handy for appropriate officials.

Opportunities for Chong's firm also abound in Europe, where the company has been active in taking down decommissioned nuclear power plants. This work is difficult because workers have to wear protective clothing and respirators to guard against remaining radioactive material. Chong is pursuing other European markets as well. Chong was one of twenty-two female participants in a Women in Trade mission to London and Amsterdam in September 1995, sponsored by the White House and led by the Commerce Department. According to Chong, the missions were great for establishing long-term contacts because they gave the participants a kind of exposure they could not get on their own. During the past sixteen years, Engineered Demolition has since grown from a family business to a business with a staff of twenty, including several project managers skilled in implosion in international markets. Through careful planning, this small company has successfully grown global with a service typically thought of as a domestic business.

CHAPTER

2

Is Your Company a Candidate for Global Expansion?

Global marketing can be a highly attractive method of increasing sales and profits. It can be the antidote to slow market growth at home and a defense mechanism for companies that are under strong competitive attack. When the attack is coming from foreign competitors, it may pay to take the battle to foreign territories, rather than fight exclusively on home territory. The needs and rewards of going global will be explored in full in this chapter.

However attractive a global strategy may be, not all companies can survive in the global marketplace, or even need to. There is little point in pursuing a complex and costly strategy if the basic prerequisites for success are not present. If a global program takes your eyes off a lucrative home market to the extent that you lose more than you gain, the effort is hardly worthwhile. To determine whether your company is a candidate for global expansion, answer the following basic checklist of questions:

- Do you have the right motivation and attitude to be successful?
- Are your company's products and services suitable for global markets?
- Do you have the financial resources to sustain a global program?
- Do you have the appropriate human resources?
- What changes need to be made to your organization to support a global program?

The contributing author to this chapter was Neil Simon, president, Business Development Group, Inc., Ann Arbor, Michigan.

Do You Have the Right Motivation and Attitude to Be Successful?

Companies that successfully globalize or realize success in foreign markets have developed a *strategic mind-set* toward expanding their business in foreign markets. Not only is this concept embraced by the senior executive or leader of the firm, but it is also clearly communicated to all employees. With a clear strategic objective, these firms expand their businesses thoughtfully and carefully, yet at a competitive pace.

Tracer Research Corporation in Tucson, Arizona, is an example of a firm that has a strategic mind-set to go global. Tracer Research, formed in 1983, is a privately held company and the originator and developer of soil sampling and analysis technology for environmental applications. The company assesses soil and groundwater contamination, conducts leak detection on above- and below-ground storage tanks and pipelines, and designs and uses mobile vans to conduct on-site assessments. Tracer Research has about eighty-five employees in Arizona, Colorado, New Jersey, the United Kingdom, and Italy.[1]

In 1990, Tracer Research was working out of a client's office in Copenhagen. The following year, the company decided to set up an office in Brussels. According to its vice president of sales and marketing, that was the beginning of the company's formal presence in Europe. The firm then moved to Florence, Italy, because most of its work was in southern Europe. It has been in Italy for about four years and in the United Kingdom for three years.

In 1994, international business accounted for about 4 percent of the company's sales. In 1995, international activity grew to 10 percent of sales, and it will probably double in 1996 to 18 or 20 percent. The increase in overseas business is the result of an intentional commitment to that business, involving increased sales activities. Tracer Research is now selling in the European Community, South Korea, Argentina, Japan, Thailand, Canada, and Mexico—and looking for new markets. Specifically, the company is focusing on countries that have tank-testing requirements or other conditions favorable to its business.

The three-pronged approach—(1) develop a strategic mind-set; (2) organize and focus your efforts; and (3) just do it—works for many small firms. But before entering into the global market, it is important that you establish the right motivation and attitude. There are a variety of reasons for owners of small to midsize businesses to want to go into the global marketplace. Your rationale is key to your international business strategy. If you do not examine your reasons for going global, the consequences could result in an expensive business-venture failure.

Let us explore your attitudes and assumptions, beliefs and motivations. A company's entry into the export or import world needs to tie into its owner's (or senior-level executive's) personal and business goals. First, you must accept the fact that taking the firm into the worldwide marketplace is critical for the firm's survival, growth, and economic health in the future. Without this top-down vision for your business, it will be difficult for the rest of the firm to execute and commit to the global expansion effort. This effort is major and will require your personal commitment. It is not a part-time effort.

Second, you need to understand the demands that will be placed on you, and you need to be willing to meet those needs. Going global is not just a matter of taking a product that works in one culture and shipping it to another. Third, going global may change the organization of your firm. You must be prepared to make these changes. Fourth, going global will involve assuming financial risks. You must be prepared, mentally and financially, for these risks.

Going global is a big step. Your mind-set needs to be prepared for the total program. Even if you plan to export products to only one or two countries, you must be prepared for a multinational effort. International business means just that—international business in international markets. It is rare for a company to export to only one country or to only one market. Most successful companies have products with exportability to several countries.

Are Your Company's Products and Services Suitable for Global Markets?

As a senior executive of a small- or middle-market firm or a business owner, you need to think through the issue of global expansion in terms of the following questions:

- **Do you have a product or service that other cultures need?** You may perceive that another country needs your products or services. But in most cases, those products or services will have to be adapted to the local culture. You will have to do your homework to determine whether the country has a similar or competitive product or not and what modifications you may need to make to your product. There is no substitute for market analysis.

- **Can your products be successfully distributed, sold, and advertised in other countries?** Answering this question also requires market analysis and internal research. Although demand for your products may appear to be strong in select countries, you may encounter obstacles to distribution, legislation, tariffs, and local competitive products. Many international product failures are due to cultural biases and marketing mistakes. You must take care to avoid the blunders that arise from a failure to understand the variations in need among cultures.

- **Do you have the skills to develop personal relationships in other countries?** The personal relationships that are required to sustain an international business are harder to form but tend to be more durable. This is because of both the mystique of dealing with international clients and suppliers and the additional "kick" that comes from doing business in foreign countries, and also because the products or services can gain additional luster because they emanate from a foreign source. The enhancement may be more to do with image than fact, but is no less powerful. Does Evian water really taste better or provide more minerals than spring water from New Hampshire, or is it the French origin that adds attraction? Paradoxically, the French, who take their water seriously, could possibly be persuaded to develop a preference for New Hampshire spring water because of its American origins! The fact that products from foreign sources commonly attract a price premium demonstrates the additional hold they can possess over customers. A foreign source advantage does not just happen, it has to be created and sustained. This requires considerable personal skill, especially when setbacks occur. Rebuilding Perrier's international market position following the withdrawal of contaminated water from the market in 1992 took a level of skill and dedication well beyond that required for conventional marketing.

- **Are you personally prepared to get involved in your firm's global expansion effort?** You, your senior staff members, and your employees down to the lower-level administrative positions will become international representatives of your products and services. Whether negoti-

EXHIBIT 2–1 ▪ MARKET OPPORTUNITIES IN DEVELOPED COUNTRIES

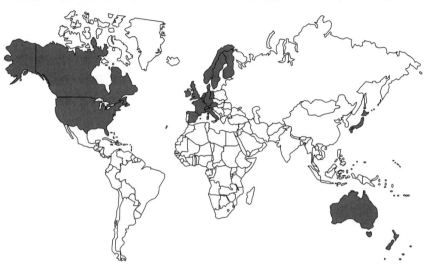

POTENTIAL MARKET OPPORTUNITIES

Software and network systems
Voice and data technology
Ethnic markets
Health-care programs
Global branded consumer products
Cable television
Financial consulting services
Leisure and sports products
Tourism

COUNTRIES

Australia
Canada
Japan
New Zealand
Western and Northern Europe
United States of America

Source: SIS International Research.

ating high-level agreements, demonstrating the products, or processing letters of credit or invoices, the members of your firm will be the ambassadors of your products. You must plan for this effort and be prepared to involve yourself directly with such activities as marketing, international production or distribution, the creation of unique personalized products, and international trade conferences and meetings.

Whether you think this effort is worthwhile will depend on your perception of the scale of the opportunity. Exhibits 2-1, 2-2, and 2-3 outline

EXHIBIT 2-2 ■ MARKET OPPORTUNITIES IN DEVELOPING COUNTRIES

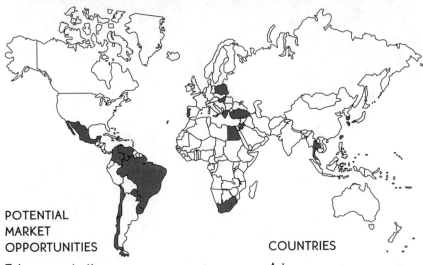

POTENTIAL MARKET OPPORTUNITIES

Telecommunications
Information systems
Waste water systems
New oil refineries
Cable television entertainment
Transportation/superhighways
Natural gas pipeline systems
Environmental technology
Nuclear, coal, electric, and hydro power
Medical instruments
Electronic components
Automotive parts
Distribution channels
Financial consulting services
Computers and peripherals
Tourism
Aircraft and parts
Laboratory scientific instruments

COUNTRIES

Asia
South Korea
Taiwan
Thailand
Eastern and Southern Europe
Czech Republic
Greece
Hungary
Poland
Portugal
Latin America
Brazil
Chile
Colombia
Mexico
Venezuela
Africa and Middle East
Egypt
Israel
South Africa
Turkey

Source: SIS International Research.

EXHIBIT 2-3 ■ MARKET OPPORTUNITIES IN EMERGING-GROWTH COUNTRIES

POTENTIAL MARKET OPPORTUNITIES

Health care
Transportation infrastructure
Consumer products
Consumer durables
Education
Automation
Manufacturing equipment
Water Purification systems
Food and packaged goods
Telecommunications
Computers
Apparel
Agricultural chemicals
Financial consulting services
Energy sector
Aircraft and parts
Grains
Building and construction

COUNTRIES

Asia
Cambodia
People's Republic of China
India
Indonesia
Laos
Malaysia
Vietnam

Eastern Europe
Estonia
Kazakhstan
Latvia
Lithuania
Russia

Latin America
Costa Rica
El Salvador
Guatemala
Paraguay
Uruguay

Africa
Kenya
Nigeria

Source: SIS International Research.

the investment opportunities by the developed, developing, and emerging-growth countries. Again, developed economies are those that have a fully developed infrastructure (transportation, communications and technology, health care, education, etc.) along with a forecast annual GDP growth rate of 2 to 4 percent for the next five years. Examples of developed regions or countries include North America, Western Europe, Japan, and Australia.

Developing countries are countries that have some level of infrastructure in place and have a forecast annual GDP growth rate of 4 to 6 percent over the next five years. Examples include Chile, Argentina, Brazil, Taiwan, and South Korea. Emerging-growth countries require a significant level of investment in their infrastructure and have an annual GDP growth rate of 6 to 10 percent. Examples of emerging-growth countries are India, the People's Republic of China, and Vietnam.

Going Global

Bottom line, when you go international, you should ask, "What's in it for me?" What are the advantages for me and my company? Let's examine the myths of going global and how these myths can be overcome.

Myth 1: Going Global Will Insulate or Protect Your Business from Economic Downturns or Recessions

You should consider global expansion as a strategy to increase the sales of your firm rather than to protect against the economic cycles of your domestic market. While this book is being written, to many of us the world appears to be in a state of reorganization. During this process new markets are emerging, and an opportunity exists for small businesses to take a place in the global market. This opportunity can help as you face marketing challenges, such as stabilizing sales affected by seasonal fluctuations. You can create new markets for your organization and establish an environment that fosters increased sales through increased repeat orders. Moreover, you can extend the life of your product by extending its life cycle in emerging and developing countries.

Myth 2: Going Global Will Increase Your Profitability and Share of the Worldwide Marketplace

This statement may or may not be true. Although most exported products and services command premium prices because of their uniqueness, local market demand, or value-added quality or service, there is no guarantee that exporting your products will increase the profitability of your firm. If increasing your global market share is one of your strategic objectives, again, there is no guarantee that globalization will achieve this objective. The Japanese have a well-documented history of increasing worldwide share of their products without increasing profitability of their companies. Do not jump on the bandwagon in the hope of achieving these objectives.

Myth 3: Going Global Will Improve the Morale of Your Company

Some companies use going global as their last hope for improving company morale. Do not fall into this trap! Best-in-class and excellent companies are born domestically. They do not achieve this status through going global. Build your best-in-class reputation in your home market and your world-class reputation in the global markets. On the other hand, your firm will be more attractive to highly educated new hires if you can offer a global or worldwide company rather than limited marketing in your domestic market.

Myth 4: If You Don't Go Global, Your Competition Will, and You Will Not Be Able to Catch Up

Although your competitors may appear to be successfully expanding their products and services all over the world, at the end of the day it is not inevitable that you will have an equal measure of their success. You will have to judge for yourself whether you and your competitors are successes or failures in these global markets. Do not be convinced by global media publications and word of mouth in your industry. Rapid reaction to competitive global moves is the kiss of death in developing and emerging markets, particularly those that require investing significant sums for market entry.

Myth 5: If You Are Not First in the Market, You Do Not Have a Chance of Achieving Market Dominance in the Country

There is a myth that the first company in the country gains market dominance. This is not true. In numerous cases, firms that have rushed into markets have made significant marketing blunders and will not be able to enter those markets again.

On the other hand, early entry into a regional market or country can give you early market acceptance and, perhaps, a temporary foothold in the market, especially when you are introducing a new technology to a country (e.g., cellular telephones, specific software products, fast foods).

Myth 6: You Will Have to Establish Manufacturing and Warehousing or Distribution Capabilities in the Local Country to Distribute Your Products Successfully

Even the largest multinational firms began their international expansion by exporting their products. Generally, a firm actively seeks foreign direct investment in a foreign country only when the following conditions exist in the market:

- After several years of exporting its products to the country, the firm has a well-established local, domestic market with strong demand and few competitors.
- The company has determined that local manufacturing of the product is more profitable or cost-efficient than domestic production (lower labor rates, lower cost of raw materials, etc.).
- Local manufacturing is necessary to obtain a dominant market share in the foreign country (e.g., because of the country's trade regulations).

Do You Have the Financial Resources to Sustain a Global Program?

This is one of the most important determinations you will make, and it certainly has significant financial ramifications for your firm and perhaps for you personally (if yours is a small, privately held firm). The possible *financial gains from going global* include:

- Increased sales, market share, and profits
- Increased competitive intelligence and improved technology
- Expanded market and product capabilities through joint ventures or strategic alliances in other countries
- Extended life cycle of your products through locating an emerging and developing market that needs the basic versions of your products
- Additional patents and technology and improved products through integration of local technologies and innovations with your products

Of course, the reality of the local market or unsuccessful execution of your globalization efforts may preclude realization of these gains. Factors that can result in financial losses associated with globalization efforts include:

- Inability to find the appropriate local representative, which can make or break your firm
- Lack of understanding of the local culture and market
- Local, domestic political and economic problems that are beyond your control
- Overestimation of the potential revenues and underestimation of the time frame for achieving the revenues
- Pulling out of emerging and developing countries because of lack of results in the short term, rather than hanging in there for the long term
- Failure to make the local and governmental contacts that are critical to long-term success in the country
- Inability to commit the human and capital resources needed to execute the globalization effort for the long term

Once you are well into the execution of your globalization program, you may discover that your efforts have several financial ramifications. For instance, globalization can positively affect overhead costs by spreading them out over more sales, which, in turn, can positively affect product and service costs, margins, and pricing. Globalization can also provide opportunities for offshore taxation and may accelerate growth and thus positively influence the bottom line.

Operationally, the global competitive advantage often means higher productivity, which can be both a blessing and a curse. Higher productivity is a blessing in that it allows for better use or amortization of your fixed assets; it is a curse in that it entails increasing personnel, maintenance, time, and so on. Greater global sales also eventually lead to lower per-unit fixed costs while making increased use of your domestic and international organizational personnel and equipment.

Do You Have the Appropriate Human Resources?

International business development or expansion will truly test the traditional organizational structure and resources of your firm. First and foremost, you must determine who will be your international leader or champion, who can execute your international development program and effort. Next, it is important to assess, or take inventory of, the human resources available to execute your vision.

What Changes Need to Be Made to Your Organization to Support a Global Program?

In working in the global market, it is important to create an image of something to which people can relate, to establish a unique, competent product or service. Global companies need to be able to relate to your product or service, and your customers need to know that you are able to deliver what they need and that your product has reliability and quality.

Several aspects of your thinking, and possibly of your organizational structure as well, may need to change for you to go global.

1. Going global is likely to mean bringing together a range of resources and skills and focusing activity through teams. A compartmentalized organizational structure is a major impediment to this approach.

2. Your compensation and reward arrangements need to avoid the pitfalls of a competitive system. You want to reward behaviors that are collaborative and involve working as a team. Global team rewards will be increasingly important. You will also need to address issues of compensation differences between nations. If the pay differential is too great, the environment will be one of competition rather than cooperation.

3. You need to understand what your customers desire in terms of a relationship. In most countries, personal relationships take precedence over improved technology, lower prices, better service, and so on. Regardless of political and economic conditions, you must be prepared to make a long-term commitment to the country and to your customers, suppliers, and distributors. Should you decide to pull out of the country, plan never to reenter that country. These strategic and important relationships will take time. If you do not have the patience to develop them, rethink your globalization efforts and strategies.

Even with careful planning and research, you may encounter the following problems in your globalization efforts:

- Difficulty finding people who can deal with the global community experience
- Failure to invest the time and funds to develop a foreign network different from your domestic market

- Lack of sufficient and suitable experience in international business to develop existing staff
- Adverse effects in your domestic operations as you create a new staff for the global activity and blend it with your existing staff
- Practical problems arising from cultural differences of employees and alliance partners
- Difficulty determining employees' skill sets to meet production and delivery needs, relationship-establishing methodologies, and marketing needs in the specific market
- Inability to meet the need for management skills that are culturally sensitive and context specific and that are not readily teachable outside the international firm or international setting
- Differing occupational practices and work expectations embedded in international labor markets and management systems
- Need to overcome managerial mental maps—of specific industries, countries, or both—to create an understanding of markets and strategic options

Case Study
Going Global Rather Than Reducing the Number of Employees

Precision Components Corporation (PCC) of York, Pennsylvania, adapted its organization to support its global program. A manufacturer of high-quality heavy equipment, PCC had been a supplier to the U.S. Navy, with 90 percent of its sales in the defense market. The curtailment of the Sea Wolf submarine program in 1992 led to cutbacks at Precision Components—from 650 employees to about 400. The company's president and CEO became aware of an opportunity to bid on a contract in Japan that involved the same type of technology that PCC used in its defense work.

Precision Components was one of several firms evaluated by the Japanese and ultimately won a contract over a U.K. company. PCC will build containers and deliver them to Baltimore, where Nuclear Fuel Transport, a consortium of Japanese nuclear utilities, will take ownership. The contract runs for two years and is valued at $24 million. Without the contract, the firm would have had to reduce employment further. Precision Components Corporation was honored by the state of Pennsylvania at the 1995 Governor's Export Excellence Awards Dinner. PCC is currently bidding on another contract with the Japanese and looking at opportunities in other countries.

Before landing its Japanese contract, the firm had not actively exported. According to PCC's CEO, the company needed a lot of hand-holding. The international trade specialist from the local department of commerce took PCC under his wing and explained where to get information. One of his most useful functions was to advocate for Precision Components to the Ex-Im Bank.

Eighteen months is generally the upper limit for repayment for the Ex-Im Bank. PCC was asking for thirty to thirty-two months because it needed to make a substantial investment throughout the life of the contract in order to pay people and buy materials. PCC's creditors in York were willing to finance the working capital only if a guarantee was obtained. Without that guarantee, PCC probably would have had to refuse the order from Japan. If it had done so, the company would not be global today.

———

If your company is to create a true competitive advantage, it will have to make the transition into an organization that will meet the needs of a different culture. The implications of this process are many. Your product or service must meet the needs or capacity that your customers value or desire. You may have to repackage what you have to address cultural variables. Your offering must meet the key purchasing criteria for each market you pursue. Understanding the value differences among cultures is critical to the success of your venture.

It is often difficult to communicate your competency and the related competitive advantages to the foreign market. We have all heard of companies that have stumbled in their attempts to make this communication. Your prospect needs to be aware of your product to be able to determine your specific competencies and advantages.

A study by Stoner identified areas of distinctive competence for small businesses and assessed the degree to which those competencies can lead to competitive advantage and sustainable competitive advantage. Exhibit 2-4 addresses the issues of key buying criterion, communication, potential for competitive advantage, and sustainability.[2]

The bottom line in the development of a successful organization is ensuring that your organization can respond to your customers' needs. To do so, you need to develop flexibility within your organization and be able to work in partnership by forming strategic alliances with other businesses so that each is helped in its success.

EXHIBIT 2-4 ■ STAGES OF THE ORGANIZATIONAL LIFE CYCLE

AREA OF DISTINCTIVE COMPETENCE	KEY BUYING CRITERION	COMMUNICATION	POTENTIAL FOR COMPETITIVE ADVANTAGE	SUSTAINABILITY
Experience/knowledge/ skill of owners/workers	Only if directly reflected in final product or service	May be difficult to establish	Moderate to low	Generally strong
Unique/special/original product or service	Yes, particularly if geared to unmet consumer needs	Relative ease	High	Depends on competition
Better/more complete customer service	Yes, unless price is adversely affected	May be difficult to establish	Moderate	Generally strong
Location	Depends on nature of product/service	Direct and straightforward	Moderate to high	Strong
Low costs/price	Yes	Relative ease	High	Depends on size and strength of competition, ability to undercut prices
Variety/availability/ flexibility of product/ service	Yes	Relative ease	High	Generally strong

Continued

EXHIBIT 2-4 ■ Continued

AREA OF DISTINCTIVE COMPETENCE	KEY BUYING CRITERION	COMMUNICATION	POTENTIAL FOR COMPETITIVE ADVANTAGE	SUSTAINABILITY
Relative quality of product/service	Yes, unless price is higher than additional value quality provided	May be difficult to establish	Moderate	Strong
Friendly atmosphere	Only if reflected through other factors (e.g., better service)	May be difficult to establish	Low to moderate	Generally strong
Reputation/image	Yes, unless price is adversely affected	May be difficult to establish	Moderate	Generally strong
Unique method of marketing	Yes, if the approach is important to consumer (e.g., convenience, speed, etc.)	Relative ease	High	Generally strong
Reaching a unique market niche/untapped market	Yes	Relative ease	High	Strong

Source: H. Robert Dodge, Sam Fullerton, and John E. Robbins, "Stage of the Organizational Life Cycle and Competition as Mediators of Problem Perception of Small Businesses," *Strategic Management Journal* 15 (1994): 121–134.

Case Study
Success Story: We Are Going After Relationships

Smith and Nephew Orthopaedics designs and manufactures total orthopedic implants that are reused for total joint replacement of knees, hips, and shoulders. The company also designs and manufactures products used for trauma applications—pins, rods, screws, plants—and products for treatment of spinal conditions, for example, degenerated spinal disks, which are also implants. The company has 1,500 employees at its headquarters and manufacturing facilities in Memphis, Tennessee, and its regional sales offices throughout the country. In the orthopedics industry, 50 percent of sales are in the United States, and the remaining 50 percent are all over the world. Japan is the largest export market.

In 1991, Smith and Nephew Orthopaedics wanted to visit Japan to meet with researchers in the private sector or government who could help the company locate people working in areas of interest to it. The company approached staff in the U.S. Department of Technology Administration who helped identify several academic researchers and some officials in Japan's Ministry of International Trade and Industry. Smith and Nephew Orthopaedics corresponded with those individuals, and its representatives had the opportunity to meet with all of them when in Japan. The company's representatives also visited the International Trade Administration's commercial office in Japan. The foreign commercial officers had contacts in the medical industry that were quite helpful. Several other meetings were set up, and the company developed a sense as to how to proceed. Now Smith and Nephew Orthopaedics returns to Japan every year; it has developed strong relationships with academic researchers at Kyoto University and with several high-tech biomedical companies.

Its contacts with the Technology Administration helped Smith and Nephew Orthopaedics gain access to other Washington agencies, primarily the State Department and the National Academy of Sciences, which resulted in further involvement in its areas of interest. The National Technical Information Service (NTIS), which publishes federal technical data, collaborates with its counterpart in Japan, the JICST, and annually sponsors a conference on the exchange of information.

These meetings put Smith and Nephew Orthopaedics' staff in contact with technology information managers. Through increased familiarity with the community and how it works, the company has better access to technical developments in Japan.

This company started from ground zero, with no knowledge of international markets. It recommends asking your local department of commerce for assistance in going after relationships because the staff has knowledgeable connections.

Knowledge About Organizational Growth

To grow your organization into a global organization, you need to understand some fundamental concepts about small business growth. In his work, Neil Churchill[3] characterizes the five stages of small business growth by addressing the main problems and questions faced by the organization at each stage and applying the information gathered to the five fundamental managerial factors: management style, organizational structure, formal systems, major strategic goals, and owner's involvement. A summary of Churchill's five stages of organizational development of small firms is provided in Appendix I. Another important piece of knowledge is understanding the stages of the organizational life cycle and competition, which can help predict and mediate problems of small businesses. These stages are summarized in Exhibit 2-5.

Knowledge About Resources

What resources (financial, operational, human) do you need in order to go global? There are three key areas that need exploring.

First, adequate financial resources are critical to the success of going global. Financial resources include cash and borrowing power. You need to fund this operation for both the short and the long term. Your marketing, sales, and advertising expenses may significantly increase depending where you want to conduct business. Operational expenses, such as communications and personnel, will also increase. For instance, significant time differences between locations may mean hiring more personnel for different times of day. ISO certification is required for many types of businesses.

EXHIBIT 2-5 ■ ORGANIZATIONAL LIFE CYCLE

EARLY STAGES	LATE STAGES
LITTLE OR NO COMPETITION	
Lack of dependencies and constraints in pursuing goals	Environment neither threatening nor constraining
Critical problems: resources, marketing approach, formalization of structure, market acceptance	*Critical problems:* stabilizing the firm's position, formalization and control
Problems and concerns: Market knowledge, market planning, location, product issues	*Problems and concerns:* Market knowledge, location
INTENSE COMPETITION	
Turbulent environment, action of competitors may constrain	Muddling behaviors, simply reacting
Critical problems: identifying niches, monitoring competition, realignment of the organization vis-à-vis competition	*Critical problems:* maintaining market position; furthering image via differentiation and focus strategy, cost control
Problems and concerns: Market knowledge, adequate capital, expansion	*Problems and concerns:* competitors, product issues, inventory control, facilities and equipment

Source: H. Robert Dodge, Sam Fullerton, and John E. Robbins, "Stage of the Organizational Life Cycle and Competition as Mediators of Problem Perception of Small Businesses," *Strategic Management Journal* 15 (1994): 121–134.

Second, your operational resources need to be developed to enhance your ability to produce product to meet specific foreign customer needs and standards. Your management and production and control systems need to be developed as well. Additional systems that may need to be built include systems for customer support, multilingual customer relations, product-line support, support for new supplies, manufacturing and service delivery and distribution processes, thus ensuring technological compatibility.

The final resource area to consider is human resources. This area presents numerous challenges. Operating on a global basis means that you need to relate to several types of people from several different parts of other organizations. Training, performance expectations, and work processes vary greatly from country to country. Personnel management differs in each culture as well.

The Global Marketing Audit

Going global represents a tantalizing opportunity, but it is not for everyone. For every company that has the potential to market its products internationally, there are many more that would have to undergo such radical change to be successful that the effort would be unlikely to be worthwhile. Sifting out the companies that have a reasonable chance of making it to the starting block is the subject of this chapter.

Entry into the global marketplace is a form of diversification and needs to be treated just as carefully as consideration of a new product or a new market sector. When diversification was popular, strategies usually involved developing in an area that built on strengths and created opportunities while helping to correct weaknesses and avoid threats. This approach is no less valid for the geographical diversification implied in going global. The key elements you need to be a global player are:

- A strong product or service that is capable of exploiting global markets
- The technical, financial, and human resources to be a serious player in the global marketplace
- The will to initiate and sustain a global marketing program

Products, services, and resources may be a limitation, but they are rarely a critical one. Products and services that would be difficult to sell to customers outside a specific region or country are the exception rather than the rule. There are rather more cases of companies that do not have, and cannot obtain, the resources to operate globally. But the biggest limitation to globalization is the lack of will to engage in and drive a global marketing program. In the 1970s the Irish government, which has a highly effective and envied export marketing support program, found that most of its support was going to a relatively small group of Irish companies and international companies that had located a manufacturing base in Ireland. The government commissioned a research exercise to determine whether more companies could be persuaded to export and what types of support they would require. The answer was painful in its simplicity. Companies that were not already exporting did not want to do so. They were happy to devote all their energies to meeting the needs of the Irish market (or in some cases the market in Kerry or Cork or Donegal); they were satisfied with the income they could make and did not want their lifestyle upset by the added aggravation of traveling or dealing with the peculiarities of overseas customers. Global marketing is a lifestyle of its own, and it is certainly not a routine that appeals to everybody.

Nevertheless, like many companies, yours may be prepared to sacrifice a cozy lifestyle for the rewards that can arise from a successful global marketing program. The task is not to galvanize your company into action, but to set it on a path that will result in success, rather than in millions of dollars wasted on travel, overseas promotions, and local expenses. Too many would-be global marketers shoot from the hip, lured by the glamour of an overseas trip and the mirage of an opportunity.

The Mexican Export Development Council, which, like its counterpart in Ireland, organizes subsidized overseas trips for potential exporters, set up a mission to Japan. A manufacturer of Mexican furniture signed up, thinking that the size of the Japanese population and high average-income levels would translate into a substantial market for furniture. His assumption was correct, but when he exited Narita Airport and saw his first Japanese houses and apartments he realized that the massive, solid-oak furniture typical in Mexico was not entirely compatible with tiny apartments and houses made of wood and flimsy screens. A modicum of research would have saved him and the Mexican government the cost of the fare.

The precursor to any expenditure and effort in global marketing must be the *global marketing audit*. This is the keystone of your analysis, designed to determine whether your company has what it takes to succeed in the most difficult marketing environment likely to be encountered. In an ideal world, the audit should be carried out in a series of stages that cover:

- The internal resource audit
- The audit of resource requirements
- Definition of the resource gap

Of course, the ideal world does not exist. Moreover, it would be foolish to think that a company servicing a local market could, in one bound, spring onto the global stage. The process is more likely to lurch forward in a succession of initiatives prompted by opportunities, followed by tactical retreats as some of the initiatives prove fruitless. None of the big global names have moved smoothly into global operations. What differentiates them from their smaller counterparts, is a global intent and a global strategy to implement that intent. Without this framework, these large companies would not have succeeded, nor will small or midsize firms.

The audit is critical because any strategy that stretches your company beyond its current and reasonably acquirable capabilities is unlikely to be workable. The resource audit is the first, critical step in building an awareness of what your company can be expected to achieve.

The Internal Resource Audit

Like charity, a global marketing audit must start at home. It is designed to determine what your company already has going for it and will therefore form the basis for decisions relating to the scale and direction of the global marketing program and the nature of any additional resources that will be required in order to implement the program. Most companies underestimate their current resources and have access to far more than they think. Most companies also have a tendency to be overambitious in what they think they can achieve, particularly in the short term.

Who Should Participate?

An audit covers physical resources, intangibles (such as experience), information, and, above all else, people. Going global is no minor development. In view of the implications of the audit, the prime mover must be the chief executive or, in smaller companies, the owner. Only the top executive has the authority to sanction the budget and the developments required to go global. More to the point, if the person at the top is not fully behind the initiative virtually from its inception, it will never happen.

An initiative of this scale needs to be handled outside the day-to-day running of the company. This requirement may be a severe constraint in small organizations that run on a lean staffing plan and are not staffed beyond their operational requirements. The problem is aggravated because any staff involved must have the knowledge and the experience to see what is relevant and to produce an authoritative report that is not open to challenge. Delegating a junior staff member or a student who is gaining work experience to the task will invariably waste time. They will produce reams of paper that will remain unread and ignored. So, we have the inevitable catch-22; the task needs to be done, but no one who is capable of doing it can be made available for a sufficient period of time. The problem can be solved simply and effectively by appointing a consultant. Although expensive, consultants are there only for the specific task of carrying out the audit and making recommendations. Also, they can import experience of global markets and global marketing that your company is unlikely to have available in-house. Above all, they will be objective. Consultants have no vested interest in whether you go global or not and will relate the situation as they see it, warts and all.

If consultancy fees are regarded as too high a price to pay, there is no alternative to releasing management time to carry out the audit. As a break from routine, the task might be welcome, even to senior managers. They have a significant advantage over consultants in that they know the company and its business and can therefore shorten the learning curve.

What Should the Audit Cover?

Although the product audit is a major component, most organizations fail to realize that a winning product is insufficient to guarantee success on its own. In the search for assets that can be exploited, a global marketing audit must cover every aspect of your company and its business, including:

- Products
- Manufacturing
- Sales and distribution
- Promotion
- Service and support
- Image and reputation

- Market history
- Customers
- Personnel
- Attitudes
- Competition
- Finance

Products

Taking an unbiased look at your products to determine whether demand outside your own market is sufficient to justify the effort is the first, and the most difficult, step in the process of establishing the feasibility of a global marketing strategy. Although larger organizations develop products specifically for foreign markets, those embarking on a global marketing strategy must initially work with what they have. The process is complicated by several factors. First, it is difficult to be objective about something you spend your working life with and it is therefore hard to understand that foreign buyers may not greet you with enthusiasm equal to that of customers in your home market. Second, there is often insufficient information on which to base a realistic assessment of your product's acceptability to foreign buyers. Although a high proportion of personal, business, manufacturing, and institutional needs are the same the world over, the ways in which those needs are met may be far from similar. A product that is a winner in the home market can be totally unacceptable in foreign markets. Many factors, cultural and regulatory, can limit product acceptability, including local tastes, operating conditions, working practices, standards, health and safety legislation, and labor laws.

Some countries make a determined effort to protect locally manufactured products from foreign competition. In these days of free trade agreements, the restrictions are subtle rather than blatant, but they are no less effective. Food, pharmaceuticals, electrical products, industrial machinery, and automobiles are all subject to local regulation, which can mean that either significant modifications are required to make the products suitable for sale or the manufacturers must comply with long and costly test and certification procedures.

The process is more complicated by a perversity that dictates that, whereas many products are unacceptable internationally because they have strong local characteristics, many more have widespread international appeal precisely *because* they are idiosyncratic and representative of a specific local or national culture. Within the automobile market the Volkswagen Beetle, the Citroen 2CV, and the Morris Minor were never likely candidates for international success. Yet all achieved cult status in some markets, which, had it occurred in time, could have prolonged their life cycles by many years.

The acceptability of your product for global markets will not be established fully at the audit stage. For now you should be concerned with the basics and with the identification of conditions that would definitely preclude international success. The following key questions should be addressed in the internal audit:

- What are your product's specifications?
- To what extent are these specifications genuinely unique?
- If no unique aspects exist, can they be created?
- How technologically advanced is your product?
- What is the in-service reliability of the product?
- What types of malfunctions are typically experienced?
- How is the product styled?
- Is the style likely to be acceptable outside your local market?
- Where does the product sit in its developmental life cycle?
- What range of products do you offer? Is your company a specialist, niche, or general supplier?
- What specific benefits are claimed for the product?
- What are the product's deficiencies?
- Does your product have attributes that were designed for unique applications or for specific customers?
- How do the specifications compare with those of competitive products (national and international)?
- What applications is the product used for?
- How easy or difficult is it to change the product specifications?
- What is the cost of changing specifications?
- With what local, international, and foreign national standards do the products comply?

Manufacturing

The product audit should be matched by an audit of manufacturing. The primary concern is with processes, technology, and costs, to determine whether there is likely to be any competitive advantage in international markets. If the product itself has no unique advantages, uniqueness can be created through superior manufacturing; this approach normally translates into a cost advantage, but can give rise to other benefits.

In the 1960s and 70s, traditional clay drainage pipes were increasingly being replaced by plastic pipes. Although they had been used for centuries, clay pipes were at the end of their product life cycle. They could be produced only in batches and in short lengths. Installation was labor intensive, as the pipes had to be cemented together in the ground to create a drain. Plastic pipes had the major advantage of being lightweight; also, they came in long lengths, were flexible, and did not require cementing together. They were therefore considerably easier and cheaper to lay.

The demise of the clay pipe seemed certain until Hepworth, a British manufacturer of building products, spent considerable funds to develop a continuous clay-pipe manufacturing process, which resulted in the traditional material's being available in longer lengths and simpler to install using a proprietary plastic joint. The process was developed at a time when environmentalists in some countries were expressing considerable concern about the volume of plastic being buried in the soil. Clay had the perceived advantage of being a natural material and once it could be laid cost-effectively, the march of plastic into the drainage market was slowed, if not arrested. Hepworth's unique manufacturing technology gave it a competitive advantage not only in the United Kingdom, but also in continental Europe, where concerns about plastic were even more pronounced.

The key questions to be addressed with respect to manufacturing are:

- What manufacturing technology is used?
- How unique is the manufacturing technology?
- Is the manufacturing technology proprietary to your company?
- What advantages does it offer in terms of product specifications?
- Does it give a manufacturing cost advantage?
- How does it compare with competitive manufacturing technologies?

Sales and Distribution

A hard look at the sales and distribution methods that are used and the extent to which they are critical in the marketing process will pay early dividends in the assessment. It is entirely possible that the sales and distribution process that has facilitated success in your home market cannot be replicated abroad, either because it does not exist there or because it is inadequate for the task.

Another issue of critical importance is the cost of shipping the product and the relationship between shipping costs and selling prices. This analysis will determine the extent to which your home manufacturing base can be used to service global markets or whether production facilities in foreign markets have to be established or acquired. Many global companies supply low-value or bulky products that would be prohibitively expensive to transport over long distances (such as cement, bricks, concrete panels and pipe), but the structure of their global operations is radically different from that of suppliers of high-value-added items that can be shipped over long distances.

The sales and distribution audit should cover the following questions:

- How are inquiries for the product initiated?
- What are the qualifications and experience of your sales force?
- What level of sales training is required?
- To what extent is telemarketing used?
- Is the telemarketing inbound, outbound, or both?
- What amount of discretion do salespeople have in negotiating product specifications and prices?
- What specific tasks does the sales force carry out (taking orders, assisting with product selection, value engineering)?
- What is the size of your sales force?
- What supporting materials does the sales force require to be effective?
- How much time does the sales representative need to spend with each client?
- What is the normal ratio of successful to unsuccessful sales calls?
- What is the average order intake per salesperson?
- How is the sales force remunerated?
- What contribution does the remuneration package make to success?
- How dependent is your company on distributors?
- What types of distributors are used?
- How many distributors are used?
- Do different types of customers use different types of distributors?
- What functions do distributors fulfill?
- What services do distributors provide?
- What is the range of stock that distributors carry?
- What is the size of the territory that distributors normally cover?

- What delivery lead times do distributors offer?
- Do distributors need or expect an exclusive franchise?
- What types of support do distributors expect or receive from the manufacturer?
- How frequently are distributors visited and by whom?
- What sales reporting system is in place at the sales-force and distributor level?
- What is the relationship between the transport costs for the product and the selling price?

Promotion

Promotion is essential as a means of generating awareness of a supplier and creating perceptions that will lead potential customers seriously to consider purchasing. Given that new entrants into the global market need to make an impression quickly and may have no established foundations on which to build their campaign, effective promotion assumes even more importance than usual.

An audit of the promotional methods used by your company and the success of each method will provide a basis for estimating what needs to be done overseas and will also show the extent to which the promotional mix used domestically needs to be replicated internationally. It is worth noting that some of your existing promotional programs may be reaching an international audience already. The trade press is often read by an international audience, and advertising at events shown on international television is seen by a global audience.

One of the major advantages of entering the global marketing arena late is that others have already paved the way in ensuring the availability of promotional resources. Most promotional resources in current use in the United States are also available in Europe, the major Asian economies, Australia and New Zealand, South Africa, Latin America, and many third world countries. Differences among countries lie more in response to the different promotional techniques than in their availability.

The key audit questions are:

- What promotional techniques are used (media advertising, direct marketing, sales promotion, public relations, sponsorship)?
- What media are used for advertising (national and local press, trade press, television, posters, cinema)?
- What use is made of directories and buyer's guides?

- What is the international reach of the promotional media used?
- What is the role of each promotional technique?
- What is the target audience for each promotional technique?
- What are the promotional messages?
- What is the effectiveness of each technique?
- How much is spent on each technique?
- What promotional materials are already in existence?
- How easily can promotional materials be translated into foreign languages?
- Is promotion handled internally or by an outside agency?
- Which promotional agency is used?
- Does the agency have branches or affiliates in overseas countries?
- What is the role of the agency?
- What level of integration exists between promotion and sales activity?

Service and Support

The attributes of your product—its features and performance—are only a part of the assessment of what your company has to offer. Acceptability is also a function of several non-product attributes, such as customization, delivery, installation, repair, maintenance, and other support services that ensure that the product is fit for the tasks it is expected to perform and that customers receive the support they expect.

As the point of use moves farther away from the point of supply, maintaining service standards becomes progressively more difficult. The requirement for high levels of customer service normally dictates a local rather than a remote presence. There are many ways of acquiring a service infrastructure, other than direct investment, but they have to be acceptable to the client and capable of being controlled by the supplier. Sources of domestic appliances, electronic equipment, computers, and automobiles are largely immaterial to consumers because the manufacturers, whether based in the Far East, Europe, or North America, have demonstrated that they can offer high levels of service through independent retailers, trade outlets, and service organizations. The same must be true for any product that is to succeed internationally.

The following are key service and support questions:

- To what extent does your product need to be customized to meet users' specifications?
- What are the delivery lead times?

- What installation services are required?
- What are the service intervals on the product?
- What resources are required to carry out the service?
- What spare parts need to be available for routine maintenance and repair work?
- What financial arrangements normally need to be made (payment terms, credit finance, insurance)?
- What product warranties or guarantees are given?

Image and Reputation

One of the most intangible assets of a company is its image and reputation. This is also the asset that is hardest to control, because it depends to a considerable extent on what is passed on by third parties. An image is also perverse in the sense that a good image can prove very fragile when exposed to bad publicity and a bad image can prove highly durable long after the conditions that created it have been resolved. Many motoring enthusiasts worldwide believe that Jaguar cars, although well designed, are unreliable and have a poor service network. This perception dates back to the days when Jaguar customers made arrangements with their service garages to be able to have their cars at least on alternate days! "You have it one day and I will have it the next" was a common quip. Even before the company was purchased by Ford, determined efforts were made with component suppliers and in production control to ensure a high level of reliability. Today the problem is not that the cars are unreliable, but that too many potential buyers think they are.

One of the advantages of being a new player in a global market is that you can start with a clean slate and create an image from scratch. The baggage that shapes your image in the home market can be sidestepped, at least to some extent. Nevertheless, it is useful to know your starting point and to audit your current image and the factors that have created it.

The key questions for this audit are:

- What is the current image of your company among its customer base?
- What is the image in other important stakeholder groups?
- What image do you feel your company should project in order to be perceived as an effective and acceptable supplier?
- How was the actual image created?
- To what extent is the image based on fact?

- What steps have been taken to change your company's image?
- How effective have these steps been?
- Is there an image problem?
- How easy or difficult is it for your image to be communicated to foreign customers?

Market History

In business there is much to be learned from past experience. To determine what your global marketing experience could be like, it is instructive to look at how your domestic business was built up. Global markets will be different, but there may be enough common ground to provide a reasonable guide as to what will happen. The following questions are key:

- What is the overall sales history of your company?
- How were the product ranges built up?
- How quickly did sales respond to a new-product introduction?
- How were potential clients identified?
- How long did it take to convert them into clients?
- What sales messages were used?
- What messages appear to have been most persuasive?
- What problems were experienced in servicing client needs?
- What was the rate of client loss?
- What caused client loss?

Customers

Customers are the major asset of all companies, and an audit of their activities and the strength of your relationship with them is vital. In all businesses, the easiest and most rewarding sale is to an existing customer. Obviously there is a major difference between companies that supply industrial customers and those that sell products that meet the needs of personal consumers. For the latter, customers are relatively immobile, and although some international sales may arise from holiday and business travel, a global marketing strategy relies on the identification and satisfaction of new customers overseas.

Following industrial and business customers into their own global activities is one of the most effective methods of jumpstarting a global marketing program. Indeed, such customers may insist on being followed by their suppliers to ensure that their global activities are internationally consistent. This approach is common with regard to raw materials and components, but is also used for machinery, equipment, and business services. Sourcing raw materials and components from the same base of suppliers worldwide has obvious advantages in terms of relationships, standardization, and simplification of purchasing; the same can apply to machinery and equipment. When plants are owned by multinational corporations or their output is destined for global markets, competition can induce a global manufacturing standard that requires the use of comparable manufacturing equipment. Visit almost any automobile, textile, or electronics factory worldwide, and, apart from the workers, you will find little to indicate in what country the plant is located. When plant output is destined exclusively for local markets, more insular manufacturing methods and standards can be adopted.

Suppliers of business services also tend to follow their global clients. The rise of international accountancy practices has resulted in large measure from clients' demands to be provided with comparable service, in all the countries in which they operate. Standard international practices provide consistency in accounting methods and reduce conflicts between local practices and the principal practice in the home country.

Following personal customers can be an equally rewarding process. As population mobility has increased and ethnic groups have expanded, markets for ethnic products have burgeoned all over the world. The movement of American, European, Chinese, Indian, Japanese, Hispanic, and African populations between continents and countries has created local demands for specific types of foods, textiles, jewelry, appliances, and services, which suppliers have sought to fulfill. Much of the supply is organized locally, but there is a healthy requirement for authentic products originating in the home country. The biggest boost to Coca-Cola's march across the globe was World War II. Throughout the latter years of the war, genuinely heroic efforts were made by Coca-Cola employees, afforded the status of technical observers by the U.S. military, to set up bottling plants behind the lines in all theaters in which U.S. forces were fighting.

The key customer-related questions are:

- Who are your key customers or customer types?
- What is the history of your relationship with customers?
- Who are their other sources of supply?
- Within what sectors are the industrial customers active?
- What are the characteristics of the personal consumers serviced?

- What is the international scope of the industrial customers' activities?
- In what countries do they operate?
- How do they currently source their requirements overseas?
- Why has there been no previous opportunity to supply outside the home market?
- If an opportunity was offered, why was it rejected or lost?
- Do your industrial customers gain any advantages by sourcing internationally from a domestic supplier?
- What is the nature of these advantages?
- If not already active internationally, are the customers likely to go global?
- Over what time frame could this happen?

Personnel

Personnel are the key to success in any aspect of business, and global marketing is no exception. The chances that a novice company has a team ideally suited to the initiation of a global marketing program are slim, but good use needs to be made of the resources that already exist within the company. Global marketing is perceived as being glamorous, although those who do it know that this is far from the truth. Thus recruitment of a global marketing team without the involvement of existing staff members is likely to initiate tensions within a company. You can avoid this situation by auditing the skill base of the staff to select those who can take part in the global marketing program. It is common for the shape of the strategy to take account of specific in-house experience. Such experience may relate to languages spoken, previous international marketing experience, and customer contacts.

The audit should address the following questions:

- What is the job experience of the sales and support staff?
- Have any staff members been involved in foreign marketing programs with previous employers?
- What languages do employees speak?
- What in-country experience have staff had?
- What overseas client contacts do staff have?

Attitudes

As an extension of the personnel audit, an attitudinal audit can be designed to probe the strength of the intent to go global at the key levels of management. Most developments can be sabotaged by management personnel who are hostile to them; an attitudinal audit may provide a preliminary indication of a threat from within. The following questions should be covered:

- Why does your company want or need to go global?
- Does management feel that a global marketing program can succeed?
- What are management concerns about a global program?
- What effect does management think the global program will have on domestic marketing?
- What members of the management team see themselves as being involved in the global program?
- What roles do they expect to play?

Competition

The competition you will encounter in global markets will invariably differ from that encountered at home. If the markets are worth attacking, the competition will tend to be stronger also. Furthermore, competitive pressure is more difficult when playing away from home. The rules of the game may be the same, but the interpretation tends to favor the local teams.

The existing competitive situation in the home market is relevant on two counts. First, to the extent that some of the players will also be encountered overseas, especially if foreign competitors are active, an analysis of their activities and performance may indicate what they do overseas. Second, the strength of the competitive environment at home may indicate whether it is advisable to divert resources into a global marketing program and, if it is, the extent to which it is sensible to do so. International rewards have to be considerable to risk losing a profitable market share at home. Cautious players will modulate their global programs not only to take account of what they can afford, but also to minimize exposure to competitive attack in the home market while their backs are turned.

Competition from international sources can provide a stimulus to develop a global marketing program. As the barriers to international trade are lowered and the ambitions of foreign suppliers increase, there is a reasonable chance that they will end up on your doorstep, promoting their products vigorously and gaining market share. To the extent that they succeed, it may be necessary to carry the battle into their territories—their home country or other overseas markets—in order to replace lost business and keep them on their toes. It is said that the best form of defense is to attack, and the best response to a foreign competitor may well be to threaten that company's performance overseas.

The key competitor-related questions are:

- Who are your current competitors?
- What are their geographical origins?
- Which of your domestic competitors are already active in foreign markets?
- What is known of their foreign marketing activities?
- What is the geographical spread of their global marketing program?
- Which countries have they targeted?
- Which customer groups have they targeted?
- What market-entry methods have they used (direct investment, joint ventures, licensees, agents)?
- How are they physically servicing foreign customers?
- What marketing programs do they appear to be using in foreign markets?
- What share of their sales and earnings are derived from foreign markets?
- How successful have they been?
- What have their foreign activities contributed to their financial performance?
- Have their foreign activities enhanced or diminished their domestic competitive capabilities?
- Have the activities of foreign competitors changed the nature of competition in the domestic market?
- If so, how was this achieved and what were the consequences?
- What are the marketing strategies and tactics of competitors?
- What apparent advantages do competitors have?

Finance

When all else has been considered, the final determinant of whether your company enters the global market is whether it can finance the operation. The financial exposure that can be accepted is a function not only of what internal and externally generated funds can be made available, but also of the level of risk exposure your company is prepared to accept. Global marketing can be extremely profitable, but its rewards are far less certain than are those of the home market and they can be a long time coming. The key financial questions are:

- What financial resources are available for global marketing?
- What is the source of those resources (internal or external)?
- Under what conditions will external sources of financing be available?
- How long can the effort be sustained without a financial return?
- What long-term returns need to be made to equate with a similar investment in the domestic market?
- What level of loss in international markets would threaten ability to survive at home?

Analyzing the Results

The output from the audit should provide a clear and comprehensive indication of whether a global marketing program is theoretically feasible and desirable as well as indicate the scale of the effort your company can consider and the extent of the targeting that needs to take place. What an audit will not show is whether a global opportunity exists. This determination requires an analysis of global markets.

The internal audit must be viewed as a process to identify insurmountable barriers to going global. There are probably very few dropdead negatives for a company truly determined to break out of a domestic marketing straitjacket, but they would include:

- Products whose formulations or designs are so rooted in local tastes that demand for them is highly unlikely to be replicated in foreign markets
- Products that are subject to strict regulatory control and that are unlikely to meet foreign specifications without a complete redesign
- Inability to raise sufficient financial resources to fund a global marketing program
- Products for which the service and support requirements cannot be supplied locally and cannot be provided economically from the home base
- Products requiring a distribution infrastructure that does not exist outside the home market and cannot be replicated at an affordable cost
- Products or services that cannot be promoted effectively in foreign markets

The Audit of Resource Requirements

The audit of resource requirements cannot be carried out until the nature and scale of the global marketing program has been decided. Only then, and after a full investigation within the markets to be targeted, will it be possible to determine what will be required.

At the time of the internal audit a reasonable working assumption is that the resources required in countries with a strong cultural and business affinity will be similar to those required in the home market. The differences between the United States and various European markets in terms of resources required are much less significant than the differences between the United States and the Far East.

Definition of the Resource Gap

The resource gap is the difference between the resources in hand and the resources needed. This concept is critical as it provides the basis for estimating the cost of implementing a global strategy and shows the scale of the organizational reshaping that needs to take place. A major restructuring requirement could act as a deterrent for the global program or, more constructively, it could signal a need to find a partner that already has access to the resources required.

CHAPTER

4

Analyzing the Opportunities

Without thorough analysis of the global market opportunity, mistakes can be costly for the small to midsize firm. This and the next chapter provide a rigorous overview of the principles and tools you will need for global research, intelligence, and information gathering. These chapters represent the basics of international business development as they minimize the risk of global-market blind spots. Although it is impossible to avoid risks in international and domestic markets, a rigorous analysis of the global, regional, and local environments is a necessity, rather than a "nice to have" step in the process.

Once you have decided that it is feasible for your company to embark on a global marketing program, the next seemingly sensible step is to establish formally whether a market exists for the products or services offered and how it can be accessed. Use of the word *seemingly* is deliberate; relatively few organizations actually appear to recognize that upfront analysis of opportunities will save them money and speed up the development program even if initially it costs money and delays the arrival of the first order. All too many companies plunge into overseas marketing programs having made no more detailed examination of the market situation than a series of discussions with business colleagues and potential distributors. Valuable though these can be, they cannot satisfactorily address all the issues that need to be considered.

Global marketing pitches companies into one of three environments: (1) conditions may be so similar to those encountered in the home market that the marketing strategy adopted at home can be exported with minor variations; (2) conditions may look broadly similar, but differ just enough to frustrate the marketing approach that the company uses at home; or (3) conditions may be so obviously different that it is evident that a radical change in marketing approach is required. Considering that foreign markets are made up of people who speak different languages, live and work in different cultural environments, and are subject to different political, legal, and regulatory regimes, the number of companies facing the first situation is likely to be small. Even countries that have strong historical ties are unlikely to exhibit identical market conditions. The second type of environment is relatively common. It is also the most dangerous environment because it can cause companies to place unjustified faith in a tested marketing strategy, which may be exposed as inadequate only after the company has spent considerable time and money. The antidote to these difficulties is *market information.*

Preliminary Analysis

Assessing global markets is no different conceptually from assessing domestic markets. The information needs are identical, and the data collection methods are similar. The key differences are in scale and in the analytical process. Global marketing implies that the market analysis should also be global, covering all countries that are potentially attractive. Although it is possible to analyze all markets in fine detail, the cost of doing so is rarely acceptable even to large organizations. You need a process to channel the analysis toward the regions or countries or even the single country that offers the best prospects for success. The process can contain a number of sequential stages, each seeking more detailed information on a diminishing number of target markets. In this way, a large proportion of the research budget can be used to obtain the detailed information you will need to create your market-entry and marketing-development strategy.

Information is a perishable product with a limited shelf life. As it ages it becomes less accurate, especially in fast-moving markets, so there is very little sense in paying for information that will not be used quickly. In the initial stages of the analytical process the primary role of the information is one of *elimination*—weeding out the countries that are not of immediate interest. The early stages of the research process need to develop the minimum amount of information that will permit the elimination of countries from further rounds of analysis. The process will differ from industry to industry and product to product, but the steps for a typical generic approach are addressed next.

Primary Screening

The first step is a coarse screen to eliminate countries on the basis of fundamentals, that is, countries that are too small, too poor, insufficiently developed, growing too slowly, lacking foreign exchange, or culturally incompatible. This part of the process does not necessarily eliminate only developing countries. The developing world may not be attractive for suppliers of advanced consumer products, but it is a major market for basic products and equipment, such as staple food products, fuels, power supply and distribution infrastructure, building materials, and textiles. At the other end of the spectrum, cultural incompatibility can eliminate highly developed countries from the target-country list.

The primary screening exercise should review macroeconomic indicators, which are relatively easily obtained from global secondary sources. Research should include statistics on:

Population
Population structure
GDP/GNP
Growth in GDP/GNP
Average incomes
Industrial production
Structure of manufacturing industry
Structure of service activity
Construction activity
Consumer expenditure
Retail sales
Capital investment levels
Cost of doing business
Political stability or risk

Since the objective of the research is to identify the best potential markets, the analysis can be based on relative performance of countries. It may also be advisable, however, to set absolute standards and to automatically exclude countries that fall below those standards. The benchmark you should use for setting standards should be the conditions that prevail in your home market.

Secondary Screening

The secondary screening process is designed to reduce the target markets to a number that can be investigated in depth. One of the outputs from the global marketing audit will be the number of countries your company can realistically enter in the first wave of the strategy. Even for sizable organizations this number is unlikely to be more than five. The indicators used for the secondary screening must be more industry or product specific than those used in the primary screening, and therefore they will be more difficult to obtain. It would be impossible to cover all the options here, but we can use as an example a health-care product. The analysis for this product could comprise the following specific indicators of activity:

Total number of hospitals
Structure of hospital types (private, public, military, clinics, etc.)
Number of surgeons
Number of patients treated annually
Number of patient days in hospitals
Trends in patients treated and patient days
Number of procedures
Annual expenditure on health care
Trends in health-care expenditure
Current and planned investment in health-care facilities
Annual sales of pharmaceuticals

The analysis can be elaborated and refined according to the product or service being considered. The limiting factor is that, as with the primary screening, the data should be available from the types of secondary sources compiled and published by the relevant entities the world over, in this example, health ministries.

Detailed Market Analysis

The next stage in the process is a detailed analysis of the characteristics of the market in the top-priority countries that emerged from the secondary screening exercise.

Data should be collected on target overseas markets to address several key questions:

- Is your product or service likely to be acceptable without modification? If modifications are required, what should be done to maximize chances of success?
- What prices are being paid and how profitable are current suppliers?
- How big is the market and how is it structured—by customer type, region, or price levels?
- How is the market changing?
- How is the market segmented?
- What distribution channels are in existence and how do they work?
- What are customers' service requirements and how are they being met at present?
- How are purchasing decisions made and what needs to be done to stand a chance of being selected as a source of supply?
- How satisfied are customers with their current sources of supply and the offers available to them?
- Are customers aware of you and, if so, what perceptions or images of you do they have?
- What marketing communication channels are available and how effectively are they being used?
- Which local and international competitors are active in the market? How do they acquire their business and defend their positions with their customer bases?
- What facilities are required within the territory to service the market at the level expected by customers?

Many more detailed questions can be asked, but these represent a minimum. Even within this relatively simple framework, research can help solve a wide diversity of marketing problems. The following paragraphs outline the most common research applications.

Market Needs

Despite the harmonization in customer requirements that is taking place, the specifications that render a product acceptable to customers can vary from country to country. However subtle these variations, they can have a serious effect on product acceptability. For food products, for instance, requirements for sweetness, texture, color, and even smell are not identical the world over. Industrial markets show wide variations in attitudes toward the size, weight, and durability of products; some countries prefer heavy, robust items, and others choose lightweight and compact items. Product tests are an essential precursor to market analysis to ensure that what is to be offered will be acceptable to customers in the target countries.

An analysis of current market prices is equally important and should be conducted in parallel with product tests. Prevailing market prices will indicate whether you are in a position to be price competitive and still make an acceptable level of profit. Price differentials between countries can cause pleasant and unpleasant surprises. U.S. clothing and appliance manufacturers can earn substantial price premiums in the European market, whereas European suppliers of automobiles have very little chance of obtaining their European price levels in the United States. Even when there is room for price premiums, the product specifications, associated service factors, or some other parameters must be perceived as sufficiently superior to justify them. *Perceived* is the key word. Why would young Russians be prepared to pay the equivalent of a week's salary for a Big Mac—hardly part of the Russian culinary tradition—unless it was perceived as endowing some benefit beyond meeting the need to eat.

Market Measurement

A primary requirement for business planners working in all markets is to set achievable sales targets and to show how they can be achieved. The quantitative element of a basic marketing plan for your product or service will show the planned sales progression (in volume or value), the customer groups to be targeted, and the distribution channels to be used. To do this, you need to know the total volume of sales the market is absorbing or is capable of absorbing and the structure of the market. Sales data need to be broken down by product type or product category, and structural data need to show the channels through which products are distributed and the relationship between channels and customer groups. Sales targeting also requires detailed information on the customer base— who are the purchasers of your product or service, how large each purchasing group is, and what relationships exist between the products purchased and the types of purchasers.

You may know much of this information from experience in the home market. In overseas markets, you'll need to acquire it.

Market Trends

Forecasts are essential for planning future business. Information on how markets are expected to develop enables you to assess the attraction of the market, set forward budgets, and allocate marketing and promotional resources in light of the yield they may be expected to achieve.

Market Segmentation

Customer research is commonly used to define discrete segments of a market that lend themselves to separate marketing approaches. It is not easy to be all things to all people. You can improve marketing effectiveness by targeting specific market segments with the products, services, and marketing messages they find most acceptable. Segments can be defined by such parameters as geography, demographics, taste, attitudes, and buying practices, but you need research to show whether the segments are sufficiently different and homogeneous to support separate marketing approaches.

Segmentation analysis is complex, even in a familiar market, and is rarely stable across cultures. Markets that have evolved under different cultural conditions can exhibit markedly different segmentation characteristics, in terms of both the criteria for segmentation and the characteristics of the individual segments.

Distribution Research

A high proportion of products flows from supplier to customer through various types of distributors. The attitudes, practices, and requirements of the operators of distribution channels can therefore have a significant effect on supplier performance. In many markets a failure on the part of distributors to stock, display, or merchandise products will undermine all other marketing programs.

Channel research can probe the availability of channels in each target market and all aspects of distributors' operations and requirements to provide a basis for the development of effective distribution strategies. The key decisions that relate to which channels to use, how they can be motivated, and the types of information that can support these decisions include:

- Identifying the channels operating in each segment of a market and measuring their relative importance
- Examining the segments of the markets serviced by each distributor
- Measuring channel catchment areas
- Defining the requirements of distributors from suppliers in order to induce them to stock and promote products

- Identifying channel margin requirements and the tasks they are prepared to undertake
- Examining the range of products stocked by distributors and the shelf space allocated to products and brands
- Testing the relationship between channel owners and product suppliers, notably its duration, the basis on which it exists, and the conditions under which it could be broken
- Testing the effectiveness with which channels implement the service and promotional strategies of suppliers

Analysis of Customer Service Requirements

Analysis of customer behavior is most concerned with the factors that determine customer choice of product and supplier. Understanding the interaction of price, product quality, product features, and a host of service considerations, such as delivery, installation, and customer advisory services, is critical to success in any marketplace. Requirements can vary enormously from country to country, depending on what the customers have been educated to expect. The standards of service routinely provided in the United States would be regarded as exceptional in a number of European countries, where service staff tend to regard customers as a nuisance. Research can reveal the service levels expected in each country and the structure of service packages that are likely to be successful.

Purchasing Research

Information on who makes purchasing decisions and how they go about selecting products and suppliers is another core component of the marketing and promotional plan. Although the theory of personal and institutional decision making is reasonably well defined, practices vary considerably among countries and can have a dramatic effect on the intensity and structure of the sales and promotional programs needed. For example, the more formal, hierarchical, and conservative decision-making structures in Germany, France, and Japan not only form a stark contrast to the relatively informal structures observed in the United States and the United Kingdom, but also demand a greater reliance on formal introductions, personal selling programs, and good references to secure business. The study of decision making is an important component of all market-research programs, but is particularly relevant in new markets.

Customer-Satisfaction Research

To determine whether it is possible to gain access to a market you need to know the extent to which the current establishment of suppliers are meeting customers' expectations. Customer-satisfaction research provides a measurement of supplier performance and highlights the incumbent's strengths and weaknesses. Image research is closely allied in that it shows customers' perceptions of existing suppliers. Perceptions can be as powerful as reality when it comes to supplier acceptance, and research can highlight the type of image that needs to be constructed to improve your chances of success.

Awareness Analysis

Entry into a new market is facilitated considerably if the new supplier is already known and favorable impressions of the product or service exist. By the same token, lack of awareness or an unfavorable impression of the company and its products or services can increase the difficulty of entering a market. Knowledge about a supplier can be acquired in a variety of indirect ways—by word of mouth, through the trade press, or from experience in markets in which the supplier is active—and if there is reason to suspect that it exists, it is worth checking on the level of exposure and the types of opinions that are held.

Communications Research

The extent to which a global supplier's marketing program can be replicated in overseas markets depends first on the communication channels available and second on their effectiveness in each community. The availability of media tends to be similar in most countries, but the reach, sophistication, and utility of each medium can differ significantly. Studies of the effectiveness of individual marketing communication and promotional techniques can provide you with guidelines for the allocation of marketing expenditures. Analyses of the effectiveness of advertising, direct marketing, sales promotion, exhibitions, and public relations show wide variations among countries based on such factors as literacy levels, readership, cinema attendance, and the quality of postal and telephone services. Most attempts to develop common promotional strategies across countries have met with little success largely because they have ignored variations in local conditions.

Competitor Analysis

The intensity, nature, and source of competition can vary substantially from country to country, and a thorough understanding of the competitive climate is essential to the business-planning process in all countries. Identifying the competition is the first step. To compete, however, you must also understand your competitors' resources, their strategies, their strengths and weaknesses as perceived by their customers, the threat they pose to other suppliers, and their vulnerability to attack. The position will change depending on whether the key competitors are local suppliers or other global companies. Detailed knowledge of competitors has never been easy to acquire. Marketing history is littered with examples of successful businesses that have been brought down by competition that was unknown or known but undervalued, as well as examples of opportunities missed through failure to capitalize on competitors' weaknesses.

Keeping abreast of competition is becoming increasingly difficult as the pace of change in markets accelerates. Competitive tension is being heightened by powerful forces that are both driving existing competitors to be more aggressive and attracting new competitors. Deregulation, reductions in trade barriers, radical political realignments, and the increasing globalization of supply all create new opportunities, but at the same time they threaten those who fail to appreciate that the competitive environment is changing and that previous competitive boundaries have been blurred.

The most basic information requirement is a map that plots the competitive environment and shows who the competitors are, where they are, where they have come from, and the resources they deploy. A typical competitor information profile will cover:

Ownership and organizational structure
Financial history
Financial resources
Key decision makers and their track records
Staff resources
Production resources and locations
Product lines and portfolios
Patents, licenses, and other unique assets
Markets and segments serviced
Distribution channels
Export activity and countries supplied
Sales and marketing activities

The profile can be extended by probing each competitor's image, reputation, and strengths and weaknesses among customers.

Marketing Infrastructure Research

The infrastructure required to service the market effectively is a function of the service levels expected by customers and the facilities provided by competitors, and it depends also on what is available from intermediaries, such as agents, distributors, and subcontractors. Markets that are too small to justify full subsidiary organizations tend to be well supplied with agents who act on behalf of foreign suppliers. Markets that have high local content requirements tend to have spawned subcontractors who can provide the required amounts of local resources to complete contracts. You can use research to identify the availability and characteristics of potential local partners.

Researching Global Markets

Market research is commonly associated with weighty statistical exercises that take months to complete and produce reams of impenetrable tabular material. Although much research is like this, it does not have to be. When it comes to the analysis of global markets, the large-scale survey approach is not always appropriate. The type and scale of any research exercise must be tailored to the task it is seeking to address and the amount at risk. Although large-scale research exercises are justified in some situations, in others, a minimal approach is adequate. The research industry offers a wide variety of packages in order to meet all information needs. Customized research programs include:

- Survey research
- Business intelligence

    Off-the-shelf research packages cover:

- Continuous panels
- Retail audits
- Omnibus surveys
- Syndicated research
- Published research

Off-the-shelf research packages offer instant information at a cost normally lower than that of a comparable customized research program. Yet off-the-shelf packages rarely meet all of a company's requirements and often need to be supplemented or replaced by customized research carried out according to the client's specification.

Survey Research

Survey research involves the systematic application of representative sampling, questionnaire design, information collection, and statistical analysis techniques to obtain data that describe aspects of a market in the detail required by the research user. The size of the sample, and hence the overall cost of the research, is determined by a combination of factors, including the structure of the market being examined and the level of detail and accuracy being sought.

Business Intelligence

Business intelligence is an alternative method of obtaining market information. It also uses primary data-collection techniques, but directs them at limited numbers of concentrated or highly informed sources rather than at samples of customers or distributors. The following are key characteristics of this type of research:

- Its information objectives are generally more limited than are those of a market survey.
- The information obtained may be subject to a wider range of errors.
- There is less certainty that the information is obtainable.
- The results of the research can be quick to apply.
- It can cost less than sample surveys.

Business-intelligence exercises can cover all aspects of business operations. Tasks range from a relatively straightforward profiling of the product offerings of competitive suppliers by analyzing catalogs to researching complex details on the structure of a company's production and distribution resources.

Continuous Panels

Continuous panels collect information regularly, normally month by month, from standing panels of customers selected to be representative of all households, specific groups of individuals, or organizations. One of the primary advantages of continuous panels is that they facilitate the tracking of trends over long periods of time. The most widely used panels are those made up of households or individual consumers, which are best suited to the collection of information on purchases that are made regularly. These panels provide simple data, such as information about products or services purchased, source of purchase, price paid, and incentives or special offers accompanying the purchase.

Retail Audits

Retail auditing collects similar data to those recorded on consumer panels but uses as its source a sample of retail outlets rather than individual customers. Electronic data-collection techniques are moving retail research more toward censuses than samples, but not all retailers are prepared to cooperate with research agencies. What passes through retail outlets should agree with purchases made by customers. The main difference between consumer-panel and retail-audit data is in the way in which the data can be structured and analyzed.

Omnibus Surveys

Omnibus surveys are regular research exercises carried out weekly, monthly, or quarterly with defined samples of respondents, such as motorists or mothers with young children, or with a general sample representative of the population as a whole. Clients use omnibus surveys as a way to collect information on questions that do not justify the cost of a specially mounted ad hoc survey. An omnibus questionnaire can carry two or three questions from each of ten to fifteen clients. Each client pays a fee for each question asked and receives an analysis of the responses to that question.

Syndicated Research

Syndicated, or multiclient, surveys are research programs whose cost is shared by a group of participating clients. Shared cost means that clients gain the benefit of research programs that are many times larger than what they could afford on their own. The disadvantage of competitors having access to the same data may be more than offset by the cost savings. Syndicates can be closed, meaning that a predetermined group of clients buys the research and no further sale is permitted, or open, meaning that anyone can buy the research.

Published Research

Published research can be viewed as the poor person's version of syndicated studies. Normally available at relatively low prices, this research provides basic descriptions of markets derived from limited research programs. Published research is used primarily for an initial market orientation rather than as a platform for product or marketing strategies. It is available from a wide range of publishers, who select topics on the basis of what they feel will sell or that lie within the specific area of expertise of the sponsoring organization.

Although the various types of research packages are most comprehensively found in the developed markets of North America and Europe, the research industry itself has globalized, and the major services are available in all but the most primitive markets.

Do-It-Yourself Global Market Research

If you have the time and are so inclined, the first analytical steps can be taken internally. Much of the primary and secondary screening data is available from published sources that can be accessed in business libraries or on the Internet. The range of potential sources is enormous, and the main problem is not scarcity of information, but finding a path through the forests of data and identifying what is relevant. An analysis of published sources will not answer all questions about global markets, but it can establish whether an opportunity appears to exist and the main countries that should be targeted.

The main generic sources are listed in Exhibit 5-1 on pages 70 and 71.

In detail, the generic sources multiply into thousands, which may be relevant to any particular industry sector or product group. A high proportion of these sources are in local languages, and although the more interesting features or the headings of tables in annual statistical yearbooks may be translated into English, a comprehensive search for data requires a multilingual global researcher.

The attraction of secondary research is that much published information is available free of charge or at very low cost. The main disadvantage is that sources can be highly fragmented and thus the data-collection process can be extremely time-consuming. There is a growing trend, however, to publish research reports that consolidate the data available from secondary sources on specific products, industries, or activities. Available at relatively low cost, these reports provide researchers with a comprehensive overview of a market. They digest and harmonize information and commonly add an element of primary research to support the data obtained from secondary sources. Publishers of such reports can be identified in Findex, Predicasts, Marketsearch, and other guides to published research sources.

Looking Deeper

However good your secondary research, it will invariably leave key questions unanswered. These are likely to be the more interesting questions, whose answers can be obtained only through primary research—talking directly to participants in the market, be they customers, distributors, competitors, or others who can provide information.

Although anybody can collect market information, very few amateurs have the time or the skills required to carry out sample surveys. There is also a problem of bias. When researchers have a stake in the output of the research exercise, there is a tendency to see what they are looking for rather than what is there. Inaccurate and partial views of markets are not only unhelpful, but are positively dangerous. They can lead to decisions that could not only waste money, but also result in failures from which it could take years to recover.

When it comes to market analysis there is no real substitute for using the services of a professional. If global marketing is destined to feature significantly in your company's business, the need for high-quality data may justify employing a market analyst. The alternative is to use research and business-intelligence consultants.

The best sources of data will be determined by the types of data required, the countries to be covered, and the time and funds available. If you need relatively simple information for developed countries that relates to major products and you need it quickly and at minimal cost, you

EXHIBIT 5-1 ▪ KEY SECONDARY SOURCES OF MARKET INFORMATION

GOVERNMENT AND OTHER OFFICIAL SOURCES

Statistical departments of national governments
Government departments
Company registration or filing organizations
International organizations
Trading and trade-promotion organizations
Embassies and consulates
Regional development organizations
Courts
Government research laboratories
Patent offices

INDUSTRIAL AND COMMERCIAL ASSOCIATIONS

Trade associations
Industry technical research institutes
Trade federations
Chambers of commerce

DIRECTORIES

Trade directories
Buyer's guides
Exhibition and trade-show guides
Catalogs
Yellow pages

EDUCATIONAL, RESEARCH, AND OTHER ORGANIZATIONS

Business schools
Universities
Research units of political parties
Trade unions

Continued

PUBLICATIONS

Financial press
Daily and weekly press
Regional and local newspapers
Periodicals
Trade press
Newsletters

FINANCIAL INSTITUTIONS

Banks
Stock exchanges
Stockbroker analysts

should examine off-the-shelf packages. If your needs are more esoteric, however, they are less likely to be met with a standard package and you will need to consider a customized survey.

Buying Your Global Research

However the data are to be collected, specifying and buying research involves three key stages:

1. Briefing, which sets out what is required by the client organization
2. Selecting suitable resources or organizations to carry out the research
3. Obtaining a proposal, the researcher's response to the briefing

The Research Brief

A survey is only as good as the initial brief. If the briefing fails to set out what is required, it is unlikely that the right result will be obtained. A good briefing, which may comprise a briefing document and a briefing meeting, flows naturally from the initial planning process that identified the need for a survey and defined the types of information to be collected.

The Briefing Document. A research brief must include all information needed by those designing the survey, including:

- Background information
- Description of the product or service to be researched
- Objectives of the research
- Specific information objectives
- Expectations from the research team
- Internally available information on the market
- Documents
- Thoughts on the research approach
- Confidentiality
- Timing
- Budgetary constraints
- Requirements of companies submitting proposals
- Date by which a proposal is expected
- Contacts within the client organization

The Briefing Meeting. The briefing document should be sent to companies that have been shortlisted as capable of carrying out the project together with an invitation to quote. Except in the case of the smallest and most straightforward research requirements, the submission of a briefing document should be accompanied by an offer for you to meet with the researchers to discuss the requirements in more depth. The meeting can take place on your company's premises or at the research company's offices. The former allows you to invite additional staff members to discuss the requirements, to demonstrate products, and to call for additional documentation; the latter provides you with an early opportunity to see the research staff in their own environment. This is particularly important if an overseas agency is to be used.

Identifying a Suitable Consultant

You have three options when seeking a suitable research agency:

1. Global research agencies with subsidiaries in foreign markets
2. Global research agencies with affiliates in foreign markets
3. Local research agencies in the countries to be studied

Global research companies offer the significant advantages of having an office relatively near to the research sponsor, speaking the same language, using common research standards worldwide, and invoicing in the sponsor's own currency. Their subsidiaries or affiliates usually have the local knowledge required to carry out surveys efficiently. In the case of multicountry studies, the central office will coordinate efforts to ensure that the data are consistent across countries. Local agencies are suited to the more surefooted research sponsor, who knows what is required, is comfortable dealing with foreign suppliers, and is prepared to piece together the results of surveys in different countries.

The steps in identifying potential research companies are reasonably straightforward. The first step is to obtain a classified list of market research companies that identifies:

- Their specializations
- The types of data or research services they offer
- Their skills in specific products or industry sectors
- Their size (personnel and sales)
- The countries they cover
- Some of the clients they have serviced

The most common sources of lists are the market-research trade or professional organizations active in each country and the international research bodies. Key sources are the American Marketing Association list of research companies, the ESOMAR (European Society for Opinion and Market Research) membership list, the market research associations in the countries of interest, such as the British Market Research Society, and lists made available by specialist industry groups, such as the European Chemical Market Research Association and the Society of Competitive Intelligence Professionals. Marketing magazines and buyer's guides for marketing services also contain lists of market-research companies, but they are rarely complete.

The Internet lists research companies worldwide and provides descriptions of their services. Although this list also is far from complete, you know that companies that have taken the trouble to set up a web site are at least interested in providing a service. The local embassies of the countries in which you are interested may also be able to provide lists.

Finally, known users of research, trade associations, and business consultants may be willing to provide qualified suggestions of suitable research agencies, and if they are recommending a research company, they are probably in a position to identify the company's strengths and weaknesses. A disadvantage with this approach is that research users and consultants tend to have only limited experience with research companies and may not be aware of one that is ideally suited to your particular task.

Assessing the Suitability of Suppliers. Whenever a research company is offering data for sale, either in the form of a published report, a multi-client survey, or the results of a panel survey, the purchasing process can be simplified to the extent that you can get a preview of what you are buying. You can also satisfy yourself that the methodology used was appropriate and ask other users whether they regard the results as accurate. If a survey has to be custom designed to meet your specific requirements, there will be minimal tangible evidence to indicate the agency's ability to obtain the information. Nevertheless, you can look for other indicators of apparent suitability:

- Size and organizational structure. Is the agency large enough to do the job and does it have a management structure that is likely to ensure that the survey will be on time and of acceptable quality?
- Personnel. Are the staff sufficiently well educated and do they have enough experience to carry out your study?
- Apparent compatibility with your organization. Are you likely to get on well with the staff and to be able to have a reasonable dialogue while the survey is being carried out?
- Track record. What previous experience does the agency have in your business?
- References. What clients have the agents serviced and will those clients speak for the quality of the work done?
- Premises. Is the working environment conducive to carrying out good research?
- Responsiveness. How quickly does the agency respond to your inquiries?
- Brochures. Do the promotional materials give a good account of the company and are they convincing?
- Previous reports. If offered, do they indicate that the company can provide quality information at the needed depth?

Compiling a Shortlist. Your review of research agencies should be used to compile a shortlist of potential suppliers who are apparently capable of carrying out the survey satisfactorily. The shortlist should contain a maximum of three or four agencies; any more will impose a heavy burden when briefing potential suppliers, will tend to be confusing during the evaluation of proposals, and is unfair to the research agencies, given the effort required from them in the next stages of the selection process. Furthermore, research agencies will tend to put far more effort into the preparation of their proposals if they have a one in three or four chance of success as opposed to entering a lottery involving tens of suppliers.

Although the tendency in compiling a shortlist is to gravitate toward companies that appear to have the right background, it is advantageous to select companies of different sizes and types, since they are likely to construct different approaches. It is useful to consider a variety of alternative approaches to collecting data before making a final decision.

Selecting a Consultant. The final stage in commissioning a research project is selecting the research contractor or contractors to be used. Buying research is much like buying any other intangible service; the process has a lot in common with selecting lawyers, accountants, and management consultants. The main task is to select an organization that is comfortable to work with and will deliver competent research at a price that matches your budget. The main instrument used in the selection, following the agency screening process discussed, is the proposal that the agencies put forward in response to the briefing.

The Proposal

A competent proposal should include the following information:

- A restatement of the objectives of the research
- The specific information to be sought
- The research approach, the types of research techniques to be deployed, and the numbers of interviews, group discussions, and so on to be conducted
- The methods by which the results will be presented to the client, including the structure of the written report and the number and format of meetings
- The cost
- The time it will take to complete the survey
- The research team and its qualifications
- Any related experience the agency has had

Some agencies write better proposals than research documents, but the content, format, presentation, and amount of thought provided in the proposal should give a reasonable guide to the ability of the agency.

The finished proposals provide several indicators of the suitability and competence of the agencies that have prepared them. The most important indicator is the amount of thought that has gone into defining the information to be sought and determining the research methodology to be used. Proposals that merely add a cost figure to the brief suggest that the agency has not given much thought to what is required and may not fully understand the problem. Value added in the form of analyzing the research objectives, adding questions that will enhance the project's ability to solve the specified problem, and thinking creatively about methods of obtaining the information is a sign that an organization is not only competent, but genuinely interested in carrying out the project. High marks should be given for a proposal that suggests alternative approaches with different costs, permitting you to match the research with the available funds.

Assessing Alternative Offers. The primary yardsticks by which the quality and suitability of alternative offers should be assessed are:

- The degree to which the research agency understands the marketing situation of the research user and the purposes for which the research is required
- The extent to which the offer meets the information requirements specified in the brief
- The extent to which the proposal shows that the agency has thought about the problem and has modified the approach and the information yield to provide a better overall result
- The proposed methodology for collecting information and the likely success in achieving the informational objectives
- The number of caveats relating to the methodology (vague promises and caveats may be used as a justification for omitting important items of information from the final report)
- The presentation (be wary of proposals double-spaced and printed on thick paper to give an impression of bulk)
- The amount of irrelevant content, such as standard material that is included in all proposals, but adds nothing of significance to the specific project

- The extent to which the language is clear and understandable (the use of research jargon unfamiliar to the untrained reader may be a sign that the researcher agency is too academic to relate to its users)
- Cost

Cost is a primary consideration for most research buyers. Clients are sometimes surprised by the extreme variation in the costs attached to different proposals. The cost of a research project is normally made up of a daily rate for executive time, fees paid for interviews, overhead, and expenses. In most countries, when comparing like for like, the costs tend to be very similar. Variations in cost can occur for a number of fundamental reasons:

- Executives employed on the project are at different levels of seniority and are remunerated at different rates. Even sole traders can charge at significantly different daily fee rates, depending on their experience and their confidence that they can persuade clients that they are worth higher rates.
- Interviewers have different skill levels, affecting their remuneration rates.
- Overhead costs vary according to level of supervision and quality or location of premises.
- Relative efficiencies of organizations differ. Some work on higher numbers of interviews per day and lower inputs of executive time to achieve any given result.
- Profit expectations differ.

Other factors that can cause significant variations in cost include:

- Differing interpretations of the difficulty of obtaining the data
- Data that an agency already possesses that it can contribute to the solution
- The amount of time budgeted for contact between agency and client
- The desire, or lack of desire, to keep costs low to win the contract

The most likely reason for variations in costs among proposals produced in response to an identical brief is that the different agencies have interpreted the brief differently and are offering different solutions. Before accepting a low-cost proposal or dismissing a high-cost one, it is well worth discussing the offers in detail in order to understand precisely what the differences are.

Presentations of Proposals. For large, complex assignments, research agencies may be invited to present their proposals to the client. This approach gives the agency an opportunity to stress the reasons it feels it is suited to carry out the research and provides the client with an opportunity to ask further questions and test the statements made in the proposal.

Negotiations. A more acceptable, but higher-cost proposal does not have to be accepted without negotiation. Research agencies no longer regard themselves as professionals above discussing fees. There is always a deal to be made, normally involving a compromise between trimming the methodology, trimming the information yield, and cutting the agency's profit margin.

Working with Consultants

Good research projects result from an effective working relationship between client and research agency. Both partners must contribute the knowledge and skill derived from their respective backgrounds in order to get the most from the research budget. Although it may be tempting to let the research agency implement the project without interaction (or interfering), doing so can mean less than satisfactory results.

Clients require skills in working with outside agencies so that they can make an effective contribution to the research process. This step is most applicable to ad hoc research. When information is purchased off the shelf, the client can view the findings in advance to ensure that they are what is required and interact less with the research agency; even so, if special analysis of the data are required, the research process needs to be managed by the client.

Clients can make effective contributions to projects by providing:

- A detailed briefing of the research team prior to the commencement of the research
- Questionnaire approval
- Regular progress reports during the survey
- Regular reviews of the information yield
- An independent assessment of the quality of the results

Project Briefing or Kick-Off Meeting. At the commencement of all research projects representatives of the client should meet the entire research team and brief them personally to ensure that they are equipped with all the information they need to carry out the survey efficiently and within the time deadlines set for the research.

Review of Questionnaires. Clients are not expected to be experts on questionnaire design, but it helps for them to review the questionnaires and checklists to be used in the research. Clients can make a valuable contribution to the questions themselves, technical terms, and anticipated responses.

Progress Reports. Throughout the duration of the project clients should seek regular formal and informal updates to ensure that the project is running on time and the required data are being obtained. Updates also provide clients with the opportunity to make additional contributions to the survey and to see whether modifications to the research approach or the information yield are needed. Progress meetings can take the form of informal telephone contact and interim sessions at which findings are presented and discussed.

Revisions to Information Yield. Usually once a project has commenced any change in the research specifications will incur a cost penalty. Although arbitrary changes should be avoided, legitimate changes may nevertheless arise from the research process itself. For instance, data may be unobtainable, or it may be deemed helpful to:

- Collect data covering additional aspects of the market not anticipated at the briefing or proposal stage, but subsequently determined to be important
- Use incremental data that are by-products of the chosen research methodology
- Extend the research to additional markets or market sectors not anticipated in the original approach

Initial Review of Results. An oral presentation of the findings once the data has been analyzed, but prior to completion of a written report, can alert the client to the conclusions and permit the client to make a contribution to the interpretation of the data and the structuring of the report, including specification of analysis that the research team may not have considered.

Final Review of Findings. Once the report has been written, the research team has a vital role to play in selling the findings to company management that will use the data. Management personnel should be able to understand and, if necessary, to challenge the methodology, the research findings, the interpretation, and the conclusions reached by the research team.

Assessing the Quality of the Results. An issue of paramount importance to all research users is the accuracy and comprehensiveness of the results obtained from a research program and whether they can support the decisions that arise from them. Comprehensiveness of the data is relatively easy to establish, but assessing accuracy requires a series of checks during and after the research program.

The following questions are key in determining whether survey results are accurate:

- **Survey implementation.** Was the proposed survey methodology applied rigorously and have any departures from the plan been explained satisfactorily?
- **Bias.** Did any factors or events arise during the survey that could have biased the results?
- **Statistical checks.** Can the level of statistical accuracy of the findings be demonstrated?
- **Internal consistency of the results.** Are the various sets of data within the survey findings consistent with one another?
- **Consistency with independent data.** Are the findings consistent with internal data of the market or previous surveys on the subject?
- **Consistency with management expectations.** How well do the findings fit with internal opinion, conventional wisdom, and common sense?

Problems in Global Research

National surveys that examine markets in a single country are rarely problematic. However, multinational surveys that seek comparable results in two or more countries generate significant problems. These surveys need to be planned with considerable care to ensure that recorded differences in attitude and approach reflect market conditions and not differences in the survey's approach. Increasingly, international surveys are set up, analyzed, and reported centrally, with fieldwork carried out separately in each market. This method has the major advantage of providing a common approach and harmonized analysis and is generally less costly than using a series of individual country surveys.

Despite the enormous differences among countries, research surveys are surprisingly similar in approach and structure worldwide. The issue in defining international surveys is more one of adaptation to local conditions than of adoption of completely different approaches and techniques in each country. Factors that dictate differences in research are similar to those that influence international marketing, namely, language, literacy, culture and cultural traditions, religion, income levels, stage of economic development, living conditions, distribution channels, legislation, and regulation. Separately or collectively these factors can mean that what can be done in one country is difficult or impossible to do in another, and unless they are fully understood, with the help of research, local marketing plans will be inappropriate and ineffective.

The following issues require careful consideration when planning an international research program:

- Matching research objectives to local conditions
- Matching research techniques to local conditions
- Central location, or distributed field research programs
- Availability and quality of research resources
- International research logistics
- Countries to be covered
- Cost

Matching Research Objectives to Local Conditions

Marketing issues and market conditions are sufficiently similar in the European countries and the United States that a common survey design is broadly workable in these countries. Differences in culture and business practices may suggest some changes in objectives, but if the survey sponsor needs to make comparisons between countries and therefore requires the use of a common questionnaire, these differences can generally be overlooked without undermining the credibility of the research program. In programs aimed at countries in the Middle East, the Far East, Latin America, and Africa, however, where cultural and marketing conditions vary greatly from one country to another (as well as from those in the United States and European countries), research objectives must be modified to make sense of the findings. The global marketing activities of multinational corporations have begun to reduce the differences among countries, and in many industrial markets these differences are already minimal. Nonetheless, for the vast majority of consumer markets research objectives need to take account of significant differences in taste, packaging, distribution channels, purchasing practices, readership habits, and customer attitudes.

Matching Research Techniques to Local Conditions

International research programs need to take account of significant differences in the extent to which research techniques can be deployed. Again, the European countries and the United States have much in common, and techniques that work well in one country will generally translate to the others. Issues to consider in matching research techniques to local conditions include:

- Availability and accuracy of secondary sources
- Language and translation issues
- Acceptability of research techniques
- Attitudes toward providing information
- Cultural effect on responses

Availability and Accuracy of Secondary Sources. Published data in Europe and North America generally have better coverage and accuracy than do data published elsewhere. Although international sources may cover all countries in the same level of detail, key government sources may provide census and economic data at varying levels of accuracy and detail. In addition, the quality of other local sources, such as directories, can vary enormously. Quality is difficult to predict. For example, in Russia and Eastern European countries, in which the flow of information was heavily influenced by the political situation, the current supply of statistics is surprisingly good.

Lack of accurate census data has a fundamental impact on survey design. If the structure of a consumer or industrial universe cannot be described, quota samples cannot be used. Lists from which to draw random samples may not be available or may be inaccurate. Industrial market research in Russia is severely hampered because in almost all lists of companies the telephone numbers are incorrect.

Language and Translation Issues. Accurately translating question-naires is a major problem for researchers. Words need to convey precisely the same meaning and carry the same weight in each country to ensure that respondents place the same interpretation on them. Problems can be compounded by differences in literacy levels. The solution in some cases may be to rely more on pictorial images than on words.

Acceptability of Research Techniques. Telephone interviews, personal interviews, and self-completion questionnaires are not equally acceptable in all countries. Variations in telephone ownership clearly affect the acceptability of telephone samples. In Far Eastern countries, where relationships tend to be more formal, the telephone is substantially less acceptable to respondents as a means of providing information. In Russia, people who answer the phones in businesses and institutions are typically reluctant to connect interviewers to management. In the United States, the rapid growth of voice mail has severely hindered telephone surveys. Whereas once it was possible to get through to a high proportion of respondents on the first call, now potential respondents use voice-mail systems to screen their calls.

Differences in attitudes toward street interviews and allowing strangers into one's home affect personal interview programs. In many countries, security concerns have given rise to a growth in estates or compounds to which entry is restricted. Middle- and upper-class residents in South Africa, Southeast Asia, and the United States have increased the level of protection for their homes as crime rates and social unrest have increased.

Response rates to self-completion questionnaires are influenced by literacy rates, quality of the postal service, and variations in attitudes toward completing forms. A questionnaire that might work well in a disciplined market, such as Germany, with a high-quality postal service, could prove a waste of time in another country, such as Italy.

Attitudes Toward Providing Information. In some cultures, the importance of secrecy and confidentiality means that people are reluctant to discuss any topics with strangers. In Europe, the publicity given to data protection and a series of invasion-of-privacy issues has created a climate in which respondents are increasingly reluctant to cooperate in surveys. Business-intelligence inquiries in Germany are commonly stonewalled on the grounds that they infringe on German data-protection legislation.

In some countries, the interviewer's sex or social origins may influence a respondent's willingness to participate in a survey. For instance, in Muslim countries it is virtually impossible for a man to interview a woman, and in India an interviewer from one caste would be unlikely to be able to interview a respondent from another.

Problems frequently arise when questioning relates to financial matters. Data collection can be hindered because respondents have not kept adequate financial records. More commonly, suspicion that the inquiry has some official motivation can make respondents inordinately reluctant to discuss financial matters with interviewers, regardless of the assurances given.

Cultural Effect on Responses. Culture can have a significant effect on the comparability of responses from different countries. Willingness to please, unwillingness to say no or admit ignorance, and reluctance to discuss personal matters all influence the quality and accuracy of responses.

The Strategic Opportunity Grid

Once data on global markets have been collected, your main problem is what to do with it. Weighty reports take time to read, and some form of synthesis is essential before any decisions can be taken. A strategic opportunity grid is an analytical tool that brings together data on the essential characteristics of alternative global markets and places them in order of attractiveness. This approach enables you to take into account all factors that could influence performance without giving undue prominence to limited numbers of specific factors.

A grid can be used at each stage of the assessment process outlined in Chapter 4. Relatively coarse grids can be constructed for primary screening and more refined grids for secondary screening.

A strategic opportunity grid contains six main elements:

1. Generic groups of indicators
2. Specific indicators
3. Weights
4. Indexes
5. Scores
6. Country rankings

Generic Groups of Indicators

Although there may be much common ground, generic groups of indicators must be tailored to the requirements of each business. As indicated in Chapter 4, at the primary screening stage indicators of market size, growth, wealth, competition, and political risk should be readily available.

Specific Indicators

The specific indicators within each generic group also need to be tailored to each situation. Typically these indicators are magnitudes such as population, GDP, average income level, manufacturing output, number of competitors, market concentration, and indicators of political stability and risk for primary screening, and market-specific magnitudes for secondary screening.

The data must be comparable for each country. Any country for which data cannot be obtained or estimated should be excluded from the grid. This practice tends to result in leveling upward in primary screening, but is not a problem for secondary screening, which relies on market-research data.

It is important that all indicators pull in the same direction; that is, when multiplied by the weights assigned, high scores must mean that the market is more attractive to the supplier. This requirement is generally not a problem with positive indicators, such as size and growth, but can be a problem with negative indicators, such as the existence of a large number of competitors. This problem can be addressed by modifying the indicator. For example, population per competitor (for which a large number indicates a relatively small competitive base) can be substituted for the absolute number of competitors.

Weights

A key input to the grid is the weights for each indicator. In an approach that takes comprehensive account of all factors that can determine market attractiveness, a weighting system permits some factors to have more influence than others. The weights are determined by the importance of each indicator to market attraction. For example, suppliers of food and personal products may place a relatively high weight on the size of the population, the number of people in the age groups they are targeting, average income level, proportion of discretionary expenditure, growth in personal income, and availability of suitable distribution channels. Suppliers of catering products would also regard average income, income growth, and discretionary income as important, but would consider placing more weight on the number of restaurants and other catering establishments, average restaurant size, expenditure on eating away from home, and number of restaurant meals purchased per capita per annum. A supplier of office equipment would be interested in the number of companies, numbers employed, and proportion of those employed who work in an office environment rather than in a factory.

Weights can be decided only in light of an analysis of what drives the performance of the business in the home market. The drivers may not be the same in global markets, but in the absence of other information, the situation at home is the best guide. Weights can also take account of subjective perceptions of the situation in a new market. If the market is sensitive to price and the supplier will be a high-priced supplier, competitive factors can be given high weights so that a market with low prices and a high number of existing suppliers will slip down the attractiveness scale and a market with the opposite conditions will move up.

Indexes

Within the grid, weights are applied to the primary data for each indicator. To make the task manageable, more consistent, and more relevant, the raw data are converted into a series of indexes that use the equivalent home-market data as their base. A manufacturer supplying the entire U.S. market would use U.S. population, GDP, earnings levels, and so on as the base, whereas a manufacturer supplying specific states would use the relevant data for those states as the base.

Scores

The scores are obtained by multiplying the indexes by the weights.

Country Rankings

Country rankings are computed from the aggregate of the scores for each country on all indicators.

The Case of the California Cookie

In this hypothetical example, a California-based supplier of cookies has decided that the European market may represent an attractive market for its products. The products are of above-average quality and are commonly purchased as a gift item by middle-income and middle-aged consumers. In the United States, the cookies are sold through specialist outlets, which do not exist in Europe. The company feels that European supermarket chains would provide a suitable alternative distribution channel.

The following chart, which lists the relevant indicators and their weights, presents a methodology by which a company could evaluate a particular market.

INDICATOR	WEIGHT
MARKET SIZE	
Population	50
Population in age band 30–60	80
Average income levels	90
Consumers' expenditure	50
Expenditure on food	40
Per capita consumption of cookies	100
GROWTH	
Consumers' expenditure	50
Average income	80
Expenditure on food	50
Cookie consumption	100
DISTRIBUTION	
Number of retail food outlets	70
Number of supermarket stores	90
COMPETITION	
Population per cookie manufacturer	60
Average price of cookies	80
Imports of cookies	80
Imports of cookies from the U.S.	90

After filling out a chart like this for each country under consideration, the client can use the blank template shown in Exhibit 5-2 to compare the weights in each category of the countries in order to determine which country offers a more attractive market.

EXHIBIT 5-2 ■ STRATEGIC OPPORTUNITY GRID

COUNTRIES (EUROPE)	MARKET SIZE			MARKET GROWTH			MARKET PENETRATION			NUMBER OF COMPETITORS			STRENGTH OF COMPETITION			RISK FACTORS						TOTAL SCORE
																ECONOMIC			POLITICAL			
	W	R	S	W	R	S	W	R	S	W	R	S	W	R	S	W	R	S	W	R	S	S
Austria																						
Belgium–Luxembourg																						
Denmark																						
Finland																						
France																						
Germany																						
Greece																						
Italy																						
The Netherlands																						
Norway																						
Portugal																						
Spain																						
Sweden																						
Switzerland																						
United Kingdom																						

W (Weighting): The importance of the factor
R (Rating): The rating of each country on the factor
S (Score): The rating multiplied by the weighting

International Research Logistics

The increased complexity of international surveys means that the research process must be subject to more rigorous controls if the outcome is to be satisfactory. In this sense, centrally organized surveys have a distinct advantage since they are carried out by one team of research executives. Surveys in which the research is subcontracted to local partners provide far more scope for error and delay. To assure success, a strong management team must control the survey and there must be a clear understanding of who is responsible for what. The process that appears to work best involves having a main contractor responsible for:

Definition of survey objectives
Questionnaire design
Preliminary translation of questionnaires
Sample design and sampling procedures
Pilot questionnaires
Briefing of local subcontractors
Data entry and analysis
Review of findings with subcontractors
Reporting of findings
Client liaison

and subcontractors responsible for:

Local secondary research
Checking questionnaire translations
Local pilot survey
Suggesting modifications to questionnaire and research
    approach
Local interviewing
Submitting questionnaires or data files to the main contractor

The briefing and review processes are critically important to ensure that the results are consistent and that any differences in results among countries reflect local market conditions and not differences in application of the methodology.

International Research Costs

The cost of carrying out market research varies considerably from country to country. Research costs are highest in Japan—two to three times higher than costs for equivalent services in Europe. Within Europe, research costs can vary by a factor of two between countries; costs tend to be lowest in the United Kingdom. Research costs in the United States are generally on a par with those in the United Kingdom. Elsewhere, research costs are influenced by the degree of local competition, the difficulty of carrying out the research, and the level of interest in the country in carrying out research.

CHAPTER

6

Your Options for Going Global

Today, traders have many ways to gather information about societies with which they want to trade, but for centuries their options and information were scarce. Before 1500, most of the trade between Europe and Asia went over land and only a handful of people traveled from one end of Eurasia to the other. Knowledge of faraway societies was lacking—many Europeans thought the silk they bought from China grew on trees. When sea travel made it practical for more to make the trip, old stories continued to prevail for some time. The travel diaries of John Mandeville, a fourteenth-century fraud who never left England, reported seeing in Asia men who had no heads, but eyes in the middle of their chests, fire-breathing beasts, and trees that grew sheep instead of fruit, among other things. At least ten editions of his books were published in the seventeenth and eighteenth centuries.

The first accurate depiction of the world, including the Americas, appeared in a Chinese guide to the countries and oceans of the world, printed in Canton around 1701. The book's descriptions of countries are short but accurate. The book is perhaps most significant because of what it does not do; it does not organize the world into continents or people into races. The Europeans of the time were beginning to take continents as natural, yet only convention separates Europe from Asia along the Urals, or Africa from Asia at Suez. The Chinese ignored these categories and proceeded country by country along the seacoast from south China through Southeast Asia, along the Indian Ocean, around the Cape of Good Hope, and up the Atlantic coast. They grouped together people who faced the same body of water. Thus East Africans are grouped with inhabitants of the Middle East and the west coast of

India, and the people of the "Great Western Ocean"—the Atlantic—comprise Africans, Europeans, and Americans.

This approach makes a lot of sense in terms of how we now understand the Atlantic, as an interdependent zone in which people from Africa, Europe, and the Americas join together, even if not on equal terms. It also makes sense in terms of modern biology, which tells us that races don't really exist. By not creating categories to separate Portugal from England from the Ivory Coast from Massachusetts, did this book really show greater ignorance than the Oxford dons of its day? Three centuries later, that view from the docks in Canton looks very perceptive.[1]

Once you have determined the best international markets for your products, you need to evaluate the most profitable way to get your products to potential customers in those markets. The several methods of entering foreign markets include exporting, licensing, joint ventures, and offshore production. Selection of a method depends on a variety of factors, including the nature of the product or service and the conditions for market penetration that exist in the foreign target market.

Exporting involves selling products or services to a foreign firm, either directly, or indirectly through the use of an export intermediary, such as a commissioned agent or an export management or trading company. International joint ventures, an effective means of market entry, often involve licensing or offshore production. With licensing, you assign the rights to distribute or manufacture your product or service to a foreign company through a contractual agreement. With offshore production, you either set up your own facility or subcontract the manufacturing of your product to an assembly operator.

Exporting

Exporting, directly or indirectly, is the method of foreign-market entry most commonly used by small businesses. Start-up costs and risks are limited, and profits can be realized early on. Direct exporting requires that you find a foreign buyer and make all arrangements for shipping your products overseas yourself. If this task seems beyond the scope of your current in-house capabilities, you can consider using an export intermediary.

American Cedar Industries, a Hot Springs, Arkansas, producer of cedar products, displayed its products at a trade show and was discovered by an export management company. The export management company alleviated the hassles of exporting directly, and American Cedar Industries' products are now being distributed throughout the European Community from a distribution point in France. The company reports that 30 percent of its product sales come from exporting.

The Perez family in Mexico owns Industrias La Florencia, which makes aluminum kitchen utensils (e.g., ladles, cups, plates, pitchers, pots, pans) in a northern suburb of Mexico City. Until late 1994, the firm exported nothing, figuring that a ripe domestic demand could keep it busy for the foreseeable future. But the foreseeable future didn't include the December 1994 peso devaluation and the Mexican economy's ensuing swan dive. Through 1995, the demand for La Florencia's products evaporated, forcing the family to lay off seventy-five of the firm's almost one hundred workers. The Perezes didn't have a clue how to export, nor did they have a choice. They started showing their wares at industrial fairs in other countries. It was a desperate, seat-of-the-pants move. It took a while, but today Industrias La Florencia is a stronger company and a seasoned exporter to boot. It sells utensils to Europe and Latin America and is looking to sell to the United States one day. Industria La Florencia's story is a reflection of the general state of Mexico's manufacturing sector; it has been forced to become more efficient and productive and to take advantage of exporting its products to global markets.[2]

Making the Decision to Export

If you choose to dedicate the company resources required for direct exporting, you need to implement a detailed and thorough strategy that includes the following steps:

- Evaluating the product's export potential
- Determining whether your company is export ready
- Identifying key foreign markets for your products through market research
- Evaluating distributional and promotional options and establishing an overseas distribution network
- Determining export prices, payment terms, methods, and techniques
- Familiarizing yourself with shipping methods and documentation procedures and requirements

Determining Whether Your Company Is Export Ready. Formulating a solid export strategy requires a critical examination of your company's capabilities and resources. In addition, several questions must be considered, such as which countries to target and what strategy to use in addressing import barriers, what steps to take and when, what the time frame will be, and what the costs will be, in both time and money. The following are some of the capabilities and resources that your company should have in place prior to exporting your products:

- Sufficient cash flow and financing to export your products
- Experienced personnel to handle the administration in your firm
- Knowledge of the modifications necessary to adapt your product for the local culture
- Local language capabilities to communicate with personnel from the foreign country
- Knowledge of recent changes in customs and tariffs in the foreign country
- Identification of a local representative to assist in handling your products once they arrive in the foreign country

Selecting and Preparing Products for Export. Selecting and preparing a product for export requires not only product knowledge, but also knowledge of the unique characteristics of each market being targeted. Market research and contacts made with foreign representatives should give you an idea of what products can be sold where; but before a sale can occur your company may need to modify its products to satisfy the tastes or needs of the buyers in foreign markets.

The extent to which your company will modify products for export markets is a key policy issue to be addressed by company management. Some exporters believe that products cannot be exported without significant changes; others attempt to develop uniform products that are acceptable in all export markets.

If your company manufactures more than one product or offers many models of a single product, begin with the product best suited to the targeted market. Ideally, you will have one or two products that will fit the targeted market without major design or engineering modifications. This is likely to be the case if your company:

- Deals with international customers with the same demographic characteristics or the same specifications for manufactured goods

- Supplies parts for domestic goods that are exported to foreign countries without modifications
- Produces a unique product that is sold on the basis of its status or foreign appeal
- Produces a product that has few or no distinguishing features and is sold almost exclusively on a commodity or price basis.

You should also consider the following points before preparing your products for export:

- What foreign needs does the product satisfy?
- Should the firm modify its domestic market product for sale abroad? Should it develop a new product for the foreign market?
- What specific features, design, color, size, packaging, brand, warranty, and so on should the product have?
- What specific services are necessary at the presale and postsale stages abroad?
- Are the firm's service and repair facilities adequate?

Product Adaptation. To enter a foreign market successfully, your company may have to modify its products to conform to government regulations, geographic and climatic conditions, buyer preferences, or standard of living; to facilitate shipment; or to compensate for possible differences in engineering or design standards.

Foreign-government product regulations are common in international trade and are expected to become more common. Governments impose these regulations, which can take the form of high tariffs or of nontariff barriers, such as regulations or product specifications, to:

- Protect domestic industries from foreign competition
- Protect the health of their citizens
- Force importers to comply with environmental controls
- Ensure that importers meet local requirements for electrical or measurement systems
- Restrict the flow of goods originating in or having components from certain countries
- Protect their citizens from cultural influences deemed inappropriate

Detailed information on regulations imposed by foreign countries is available from the country desk officers of the Department of Commerce's IEP unit. When barriers imposed by a foreign government are particularly onerous or discriminatory, a company may enlist the help of the U.S. government to press for their removal. Any district office of the Department of Commerce or the Office of the U.S. Trade Representative in Washington, D.C., can be contacted for further information.

Factors such as availability of resources, topography, humidity, and energy costs can affect the performance of a product or even define its use and may result in a need to modify the product. Buyer preferences and local customs, such as religion or leisure activities, often determine whether a product will sell. A product's sensory impact, such as taste or visual presentation, may also be a critical factor. The Japanese desire for beautiful packaging, for example, has led many companies to redesign cartons and packages specifically for this market.

A country's standard of living can result in the need to modify a product. Level of income, level of education, and availability of energy all help predict the acceptance of a product in a foreign market. If the target country's standard of living is lower than that of your home country, you may find a market for less sophisticated product models that have become obsolete in your country. Certain high-technology products are inappropriate in some countries not only because of their cost, but also because of their function. For example, a computerized industrial washing machine might replace workers in a country where employment is a high priority. Some products may require a level of servicing that is not available in certain countries.

The market potential must be large enough to justify the direct and indirect costs involved in product adaptation. You should assess the costs to be incurred and the increased revenues expected from adaptation (these may be difficult to determine) and base your decision to adapt in part on your degree of commitment to the specific foreign market. Two firms, one with short-term goals and the other with long-term goals, may have different perspectives.[3]

Engineering and Redesign. Even fundamental aspects of your company's products may need to be changed for foreign markets. For example, electrical standards in many other countries differ from U.S. electrical standards; phases, cycles, or voltages, in both residential and commercial use in other countries, could damage or impair the operating efficiency of equipment designed for use in the United States. Sometimes electrical standards vary even within a country. With knowledge of these differences, a manufacturer can decide whether to substitute a special motor or arrange for a different drive ratio to achieve the desired operating revolutions per minute.

Many kinds of equipment must be engineered according to metric system measurements for integration with other pieces of equipment or for compliance with the standards of a foreign country. The United States is virtually alone in its adherence to a nonmetric system, and U.S. firms that compete successfully in the global market have found that use of metric measurements is an important detail in selling to overseas customers. Written materials too, such as instructional or maintenance manuals, will be viewed more favorably if dimensions are given in centimeters, weights in grams or kilos, and temperatures in degrees Celsius.

Since freight charges are usually assessed by weight or volume (whichever provides the greater revenue for the carrier), you should consider shipping items unassembled to reduce delivery costs. Shipping unassembled also facilitates movement on narrow roads or through doorways and elevators.

Branding, Labeling, and Packaging. Consumers are concerned not only with the product itself, but also with the product's supplementary features. The branding and labeling of products in foreign markets raises new considerations:

- Are international brand names important to promote and distinguish your product or should local brands or private labels be employed to heighten local interest?
- Are the colors used on labels and packages offensive or attractive to the foreign buyer?
- Can labels be produced in official or customary language if required by law or practice?
- Does information on product content and country of origin have to be provided?
- Are weights and measures stated in local units?
- Must each item be labeled individually?
- Are local tastes and knowledge considered?

Building international recognition for a brand may be expensive. Protection for brand names varies from one country to another, and some developing countries have barriers to the use of foreign brands or trademarks. In other countries, piracy of a brand name and counterfeiting of products are widespread. To protect your products and brand names, your company must comply with local laws on patents, copy-rights, and trademarks. A U.S. firm may find it useful to obtain the ad-vice of local lawyers and consultants.

Installation. Another element of product preparation to consider is the ease of installing the product overseas. If technicians or engineers are needed for installation of your product, their time in the field should be minimized if possible. Your company may wish to preassemble or pretest the product before shipping.

Another shipping option is to disassemble the product for shipment and reassemble it abroad. This approach can save shipping costs, but may delay payment if the sale is contingent on an assembled product. If you are not sending trained personnel, your company should be sure to provide all product information, including training manuals, installation instructions, and parts lists, in the local language.

Warranties. The company should include a warranty on the product ex-ported, since the buyer expects a specific level of performance and a guarantee that it will be achieved. Levels of expectation for a warranty vary depending on the country's level of development, competitive prac-tices in the target market, the activism of consumer groups, local stan-dards of production quality, and other factors.

Warranties may be used in advertising to distinguish a product from its competition. Strong warranties may be required to break into a new market, especially if your company is an unknown supplier. In some cases, warranties may be instrumental in making the sale and may be a major element of negotiation. In other cases, however, warranties simi-lar to those provided in the United States are not expected, and if pro-vided may result in making the cost of your product higher than that of competitive products. When considering warranties, keep in mind that fulfilling them will probably be more expensive and troublesome in for-eign markets. If you provide warranty service arrange to do so locally with the assistance of a representative or distributor.

Servicing. Foreign consumers will be particularly concerned with the ser-vice you provide for your products. Service after sale is critical for some products in foreign markets, generally, the more complex the product technology, the greater the demand for presale and postsale service. This demand prompts some firms to offer simpler, more robust products overseas to reduce the need for maintenance and repairs. If your company relies on a foreign distributor or agent to provide service backup, it should ensure that the level of service is adequate through training, making periodic checks of service quality, and monitoring inventories of spare parts.[4]

Tips to Help You Export More Successfully

For small and midsize businesses, the thought of exporting can be overwhelming. Considering what can go wrong domestically, you may be terrified at the thought of your products being shipped around the world to foreign markets. Again, going global is a mind-set; it is a can-do attitude. The following checklist will help organize your thinking—and minimize your fear—prior to exporting your products:

- Assess your business risk by country
- Understand export regulations
- Create and utilize an export document checklist
- Select a freight forwarder
- Understand short-term financing
- Use credit insurance

Step 1: Assess Your Business Risk by Country

- Review the major economic drivers to determine that the economies are sound and that you will be paid:
  - Income levels
  - Availability of foreign currency
  - Currency stabilities (devaluation track record)
  - Inflation

- Identify the parts of the world that are showing the fastest and the slowest growth. Is the market for your products growing or shrinking? In what direction is inflation heading? Have the currencies in your target markets been devalued? Political concerns are as critical as the economic drivers. Examples include:
  Government structure
  Instability
  Sanctions
  Trade and cultural barriers

- Check for governmental instability, sanctions that might affect commerce, and any trade or cultural barriers that exist

Step 2: Understand Export Regulations

Regulations vary greatly from country to country. Some of the more important regulations to consider when exploring global business opportunities are:

- **Antidiversion, antiboycott and antitrust requirements.** Antidiversion laws prevent businesses from diverting goods from their destination to another country or region. Antitrust laws prohibit price-fixing and other anticompetitive behavior. Antiboycott laws prohibit doing business in countries that have boycotts in place.

- **U.S. Foreign Corrupt Practices Act.** This law prohibits bribing somebody in another country, to ensure that trading practices are equitable around the world.

- **Food and Drug Administration (FDA) and Environmental Protection Agency (EPA) restrictions.** These restrictions are intended to ensure the quality and safety of food, cosmetics, and drugs and that supporting documentation for these shipments is FDA and EPA approved.

- **Import regulations of non-U.S. governments.** Every government has its own import regulations. It is important to understand the import regulations of a particular country before becoming an export partner of that country.

- **Customs benefits for exports.** If you are importing a product to a country that will be the manufacturing site and you intend to export the finished goods to another country, you may be entitled to a reduction in duties or tariffs or you may not have to pay duty at all.

- **Intellectual property rights considerations.** These considerations deal mainly with trademarks, patents, and copyrights. Make sure that you fully understand these regulations in the countries with which you wish to do business so you can comply with their registration requirements.

- **Arbitration of disputes in international transactions.** Various associations hear and resolve disputes between importers and exporters.

Step 3: Create and Utilize an Export Document Checklist

Consult with your freight forwarder, banker, and importing company to help you establish your export document checklist. The following definitions will help you get started:

- **Commercial invoice:** The standard bill that you send out to any customer.
- **Packing slip:** A detailed listing of everything that will be shipped.
- **Bill of lading:** There are two types. The first type is used when the title of the goods is not given to the shipper, but remains with the exporter. The second type is used when the actual title of goods is handed over to the shipper; the shipper carries the title with the goods, and submits both to the importer on arrival.
- **Export declarations:** These two official documents are required by the importer to ensure that the shipment can be admitted through its country's docks and approved by its country's inspectors; contains much of the information included on the invoice.
- **Certificate of origin:** Confirms the contents of the shipment and restates the origin of the goods.
- **Legalization or special documents:** Some countries require that documents be approved, stamped, and notarized by their consulate before being sent to the shipper.
- **Postal service forms:** May be required if you are shipping or exporting by mail.

Step 4: Selecting a Freight Forwarder

When choosing a freight forwarder, make sure you have a clear picture of the company. Consider the following questions:

- How long has the company been doing business?
- What is its knowledge of local market regulations?
- Is this a reputable, stable firm?
- Does it have good finances and a good credit rating?
- What is its geographic or logistic specialty?
- What is its reputation worldwide?
- What are its automation capabilities?
- What are its EDI (Electronic Data Interchange) capabilities?
- Is the company customer-service oriented?

Step 5: Understanding Short-Term Financing

One of the most difficult aspects of exporting, particularly for a small or midsize business just beginning to export its products, is understanding and obtaining short-term financing. Some of the terms of sale are:

- Cash in advance
- Letters of credit
- Bankers' acceptances
- Documentary collection
- Open account

Cash in advance and open accounts are rare global terms of sale. U.S.-based firms may initiate an open account in Mexico or Canada; however, cash in advance is an unlikely method of payment because it often limits competitive ability. Many importers are unable to afford a cash-in-advance arrangement and are likely to request more desirable terms of sale.

Confirmed irrevocable letters of credit with a sight draft are the safest and most popular terms of sale. The letter of credit issued from the importer's bank to the exporter's bank guarantees that the importing company will pay once it has seen the goods and assessed that the documentation is in order. These terms are expensive, however. Alternatively, a letter of credit with a time draft can be used to create a banker's acceptance. Approval of the letter of credit proceeds in the same manner; however, once the goods and documents have been approved, the bank has a period of time in which to pay the invoice.

Documentary collection is potentially risky as a term of sale for the exporter because there is no guarantee that the importer will sight the goods when they arrive. Consequently, there is no guarantee that the exporter will be paid. If you can afford to use irrevocable letters of credit when exporting, do so. They offer a guarantee, directly to your bank, that you will be paid once the goods have been received. For guidance in selecting the terms of sale most appropriate for your cross-border transactions, consult with your bank.

Examples of payment methods include:

- Corporate check payable overseas
- Foreign-currency corporate check payable overseas
- Bank draft
- Airmail payment order
- Telex

The importer can send a corporate check written in the exporter's local currency and made payable to the bank. For example, if you are exporting to a company in Japan, the company can issue a corporate check to your bank or directly to you, ready to deposit in your account. A foreign-currency corporate check payable overseas is written from the importer's bank in its currency to the exporter's bank. The check is sent back to the importer's bank, which translates the currency, and on that day the exporter's bank receives payment in its own currency. The drawback to these methods is the amount of time spent sending currency back and forth between countries. Bank drafts, airmail payment orders, and telexing money can be quicker. Again, check with your banker for the most advantageous payment methods.

Step 6: Use Credit Insurance

There are two types of credit insurance: multibuyer and single buyer. In the interest of limiting risk, insurance companies have policies designed specifically for the single buyer. For example, if you are selling to a single buyer in Australia, insurance companies can insure you with a single-buyer exporting policy. If you are an exporter that deals in many countries and with many buyers or importers around the world, you will need a multibuyer policy. Umbrella policies and new-to-export policies are available, each with nuances and intricacies.[5]

Agents and Distributors for Indirect Exporting

Many small businesses export indirectly using an export intermediary. There are several kinds of export intermediaries.

Commissioned Agents. Commissioned agents act as brokers, linking a product or service with a specific foreign buyer. Generally, the agent or broker will not fulfill the orders, but will pass them to the company for acceptance. In some cases, however, they may assist with export logistics, such as packing, shipping, and documentation.

Export Management Companies (EMCs). EMCs act as an off-site department, representing your product, along with the products of other companies, to prospective overseas purchasers. The management company looks for business on behalf of your company and takes care of all aspects of the export transaction. Hiring an EMC is often a viable option for smaller companies that lack the time and expertise to break into international markets on their own. EMCs may assist in contract negotiations and provide after-sales support. They may also assist in arranging export financing, but they do not generally assure payment to the manufacturers. Some of the specific functions EMCs perform include:

- Conducting market research to determine the best foreign markets for products
- Attending trade shows and promoting products overseas
- Assessing proper distribution channels
- Locating foreign representatives or distributors
- Arranging export financing
- Handling export logistics, such as preparing invoices and arranging insurance and customs documentation
- Advising on the legal aspects of exporting and other compliance matters dealing with domestic and foreign trade regulations.

EMCs usually operate on a commission basis, although some work on a retainer basis and some take title to the goods they sell, making a profit on the markup. This latter practice is becoming increasingly common.

Export Trading Companies (ETCs). ETCs perform many of the functions of EMCs but tend to be demand driven and transaction oriented, acting as an agent between buyer and seller. Most trading companies source products for their overseas buyers. If you offer a product that is competitive and popular with the ETC buyers, you are likely to get repeat business. Most ETCs will take title to your goods for export and pay your company directly. This arrangement practically eliminates the risks for the manufacturer that are associated with exporting.

ETC Cooperatives. ETC cooperatives are U.S. government-sanctioned co-ops of companies that have similar products and are seeking to export and gain greater foreign market share. Many agricultural concerns have benefited from ETC cooperative exporting, and many associations have sponsored ETC cooperatives for their member companies. The national Machine Tool Builders Association, the Outdoor Power Equipment Institute, and the National Association of Energy Service Companies are a few examples of associations with ETC co-ops. The trade association for your industry can provide further information on such cooperatives.

Foreign Trading Companies. Some of the world's largest trading companies are located outside of the United States. They can often be a source of export opportunity. U.S. and Foreign Commercial Service representatives in embassies around the world can tell you more about trading companies located in a given foreign market.

Export Merchants and Agents. Export merchants and agents purchase and then repackage products for export, assuming all risks and selling to their own customers. If you are considering this option do so carefully, as your company could run the risk of losing control over the pricing and marketing of its product in overseas markets.

Piggyback Exporting. Allowing another company, which already has an export distribution system in place, to sell your company's product in addition to its own is called piggyback exporting. This arrangement can help you gain immediate foreign market access and puts the burden of dealing with logistics associated with selling abroad on the exporting company. Oklahoma-based DP Manufacturing's products were attached to another product and sold abroad by another company. DP Manufacturing now handles its own exports and reports that 15 percent of its sales comes from international markets.

Some Factors to Consider When Exporting Through an Intermediary. Working with an EMC or ETC makes sense for many small businesses. The right relationship, if structured properly, can bring enormous benefits to the manufacturer, but no business relationship is without potential drawbacks. You should carefully weigh the pros and cons before entering into a contract with an EMC or ETC. The following are some advantages of these relationships:

- Your product gains exposure in international markets with little or no commitment of staff and resources from your company.
- The EMC or ETC's years of experience and well-established network of contacts may help you gain access to international markets more quickly than you would by establishing a relationship with a foreign-based partner.

- Your intermediary will guide you through the export process step-by-step. Over time, you will develop your own export skills.

The following are some disadvantages of exporting through an intermediary:

- You can lose some control over the way in which your product is marketed and serviced. Your company's image and name are at stake. Any concerns you may have should be incorporated into your contract, and you should monitor closely the activities and progress of your intermediary.
- You may lose part of your export-sales profit margin by discounting your price to an intermediary. However, you may find that the economies of scale realized through increased production offset this loss.
- Using an intermediary can result in a higher price being passed on to the overseas buyer or end user, which may affect your competitive position in the market. The issue of pricing should be addressed at the outset.

How to Find Export Intermediaries. Small businesses often report that intermediaries find them—at trade fairs and through trade journals where their products have been advertised—so it can pay to get the word out that you are interested in exporting. One way to begin your search for a U.S.-based export intermediary is by looking in the yellow pages of your local phone directory. With just a few phone calls, you should be able to determine whether indirect exporting is an option you want to pursue further.

The National Association of Export Companies (NEXCO) and the National Federation of Export Associations (NFEA) can assist in your efforts to find export intermediaries. The *Directory of Leading Export Management Companies* (which can be found at your local Chamber of Commerce or ITA office) is another useful source. The Office of Export Trading Company Affairs (OETCA) of the Department of Commerce has information on how to locate ETCs and EMCs, as well as ETC cooperatives, in the United States. Under a joint public-private partnership, the OETCA compiles the *Export Yellow Pages,* which lists the names and addresses of EMCs and ETCs, as well as of other export service companies, such as banks and freight forwarders. Manufacturers or producers can also be listed in the guide free of charge; fifty thousand copies are distributed worldwide annually. Your local U.S. Department of Commerce district office can provide information on being listed or a free copy of the directory.

Locating the best export intermediary to represent you overseas is important. Do your homework before signing an agreement.

Direct Exporting

Although indirect exporting offers many advantages, direct exporting also has its rewards. Initial outlays and associated risks are greater, but the profits can be too. California exporter Bayley Suit, Incorporated, reports that 80 percent of its sales come from exporting. According to the company president, 40 percent of sales come from the Pacific Rim and 40 percent from the United Kingdom and Europe. In just a few years, exports have pushed gross sales from $1 million to $4 million.

Direct exporting signals a commitment on the part of your company management to engage fully in international trade. It may require that you dedicate a staff person or even several personnel to support your export efforts, and your company management may have to travel abroad frequently. Selling directly to an international buyer means that you will have to handle the logistics of moving the goods overseas. But the extra efforts can pay off. Iowa-based Ekegard, Incorporated, using agents based in Pakistan and Thailand, states that 80 percent of its sales now come from exporting—quite an achievement in just three years. According to the company's president, exporting helps offset fluctuations in the U.S. economy.

There are a variety of options if you choose to use direct exporting.

Sales Representatives or Agents. Like manufacturers' representatives in the United States, foreign-based representatives or agents work on a commission basis to locate buyers for products. Representatives usually handle several complementary, noncompeting product lines. Generally, agents have the authority to make commitments on behalf of the firms they represent. Your agreement should specify whether your agent or representative has legal authority to obligate your firm.

Distributors. Foreign distributors purchase merchandise from a company and resell it at a profit. They maintain an inventory of the company's products so that buyers receive goods quickly. Distributors often provide after-sales service to the buyer. Your agreement with any overseas business partner—whether a representative, agent, or distributor—should address whether the arrangement is exclusive or nonexclusive, what territory is to be covered, and the length of the association, among other issues. Kansas-based Airparts Companies has been extremely successful using overseas distributors. It employs 1,200 distributors worldwide, according to its president, with over $13 million in sales and thirty-eight employees. Seventy percent of its sales are attributed to exporting.

Finding overseas buyers for your products need not be more difficult than locating a representative in your home country. It may, however, require an investment of time and resources for you to travel to the target market to meet face-to-face with prospective partners. One way for you to identify those interested in your product is to tap the Department of Commerce's Agent/Distributor Service. This program provides a customized search to identify agents, distributors, and representatives for products based on foreign companies' examination of product literature. "The Commerce Department Agent/Distributor Search located a distributor for us in India, and we have had a good working relationship for three years," says Shirley Wright, a representative of the Wisconsin biotechnology firm Promega. Promega derives more than 30 percent of its sales from exporting.

Other sources of leads for foreign agents and distributors are trade associations and foreign chambers of commerce located in your home country and in the foreign countries. The many useful publications available include the *Standard Handbook of Industrial Distributors,* which lists agents and distributors in more than ninety countries, and the *Manufacturers' Agents National Association,* which has a roster of agents in Europe.

Foreign-Government Buying Agents. Foreign government agencies or quasi-governmental agencies are often responsible for procurement of goods and services. Some countries require you to have an in-country agent in order to access these opportunities, which can represent significant export potential for your company, particularly in markets that value your company's technology and know-how. A foreign country's commercial attaché can provide you with the appropriate in-country procurement office.

Retail Sales. If you produce consumer goods, you may be able to sell directly to a foreign retailer. You can either hire a sales representative to travel to your target market with your product literature and samples and call on retailers, or you can introduce your products to retailers through direct-mail campaigns. The direct marketing approach will save commission fees and travel expenses. You may want to combine trips to your target markets with exploratory visits to retailers. Such face-to-face meetings will reinforce your direct marketing.

Direct Sales to the End User. Your product lines will determine whether direct sales to end users are a viable option for your company. A manufacturer of medical equipment, for example, may be able to sell directly to hospitals. Other major end users include foreign governments, schools, businesses, and individual consumers.[6]

Export Factoring

Export markets offer endless marketing opportunities, but also harbor numerous risks. Unfamiliar languages, laws, and accounting practices make gathering and analyzing credit information difficult, time-consuming, and costly. Exporters may spend 50 percent of their time analyzing customers that account for only 5 percent of their sales. For many small companies, the solution to this dilemma is export factoring. Export factoring is a complete financial package that combines credit protection, accounts receivable, bookkeeping, and collection services. Under a factoring agreement, the factor purchases the accounts receivable of the seller (exporter) and assumes the responsibility for the customers' (the importers') financial ability to pay. If a customer is financially unable to pay its debts, the factor will pay the seller.

Worldwide, factoring volume grew to over $395 billion in 1996, an increase of 44 percent over the 1995 figure. Of this, export factoring grew by $4.5 billion (19.4%), reaching a sizable volume of almost $28 billion. Three terms of sale are typically used by exporters: open account terms, letters of credit, and documentary collections. There is a trade off between the terms of sale and the credit risk involved with each of these transactions. Letters of credit have a low credit risk for the exporter, but the importer must bear the administrative and financial cost of opening the letter of credit. On the other hand, open-account transactions are much more favorable to the importer but are risky for the exporter. In an open-account transaction, the exporter bears the full risk of the transaction. Although there is no way to completely eliminate these added risks, export factoring is a tool that can greatly reduce those risks.

As an increasing number of importers in markets across the globe are requiring exporters to sell on open-accounts terms, factoring allows exporters to secure those overseas sales that otherwise would be lost, while reducing the risk of nonpayment. The factor's assumption of credit risk allows the exporter to offer open-account terms to buyers. Also, the factor's ability to collect foreign receivables effectively can accelerate cash flow.

There are many benefits to factoring foreign receivables. In a factoring arrangement, you avoid tying up working capital and spending substantial time administering receivables. A factor also provides you with complete credit protection against bad debts, accepts all credit-checking responsibilities, maintains the ledger and accounts-receivable bookkeeping management for multiple currencies, and handles the collections efforts. It is often very difficult for companies to confirm the creditworthiness of foreign companies. Through comprehensive international networks, a factor has the ability to obtain this critical credit information faster and more accurately than you could. Also, many banks are exceedingly hesitant to lend against foreign receivables because of the uncertainty of collecting them. A factor will assist in speeding up your cash flow by providing working capital advances against accounts receivable, generally up to 80 percent of the invoice value.

Factoring commissions are paid by the exporter and typically constitute less than 1.5 percent of the invoice value. Interest rates are usually calculated as a margin over the U.S. prime rate. As with any financing arrangement, export factoring does have certain limitations. Many factors generally will not take on a client for a one-time transaction and typically will not work with companies that have less than $1 million in annual export sales. Factors also generally do not work in countries with a high level of political or economic risk because of their inadequate legal and financial infrastructures. Additionally, factors typically do not approve receivables that have greater than 120-day payment terms.

The future growth of export factoring will depend on the willingness of exporters to offer more competitive terms in the international marketplace. With the saturation of domestic markets, companies are looking to increase their sales through taking advantage of export opportunities to foreign markets. The most successful companies who export are those flexible enough to offer different financing arrangements to different buyers. As open-account terms are becoming more popular, factoring is a way for you to maximize sales while minimizing risk.[7]

Licenses and Franchises

Many companies have expanded their businesses worldwide through licenses and franchises. When considering these methods for global expansion, you must consider not only the suitability of your products for these expansion methods, but the culture of the foreign markets in which you plan to distribute your products.

Licenses

Licensing is a cost-efficient way of expanding your products throughout the world as you technically assign your technology or products over to another party for exploitation. Clearly, you have more control over licensing in your domestic market, where there are legal services to protect your firm from copyright and patent infringement and local legal authorities can press for damages incurred to your firm. The advantages of international licensing include:

- Low capital requirement
- Low-cost method of distribution of products
- Capability of the local licensee to modify or adapt the product, technology, or service to the local market
- Ease of discontinuing the agreement if it does not work

Its disadvantages include:

- Lack of quality control of distribution of your product
- Risk of copyright and patent infringement in countries with a less-developed legal system
- Local adaptation of the technology or product may generate the wrong marketing message
- Lack of control of hands-on management of the products or technology in foreign markets

An alternative method of licensing your products or technology in foreign markets is through joint ventures or strategic alliances. These methods allow you to maintain more control over distribution of your products.

Franchises

The term *bar test* derives from the notion of meeting a fellow citizen in a foreign tavern. A bar test is sort of a litmus test of international franchisors. If you walked into a bar in a foreign country where there were several Americans, you would naturally gravitate toward them, being pleased to meet fellow citizens in a foreign country. If, instead, a German, a Spaniard, an Italian, and an Austrian were in the bar, you would not have as much in common because of the individual cultures and customs.

You cannot assume that just because your franchise is successful in your domestic market, it will do as well overseas. Even the common market of the European Union (EU) is diverse and presents unique challenges for European and foreign franchisors. Several major franchisors have made a fundamental error in assuming that Europeans think and behave as Americans do. Although U.S. franchisors are learning, their mistakes highlight some of the obstacles to franchising in Europe.

Europeans are highly active in franchising, but Americans may run across resistance even to a product regarded as a household name in the United States. Many established U.S. companies have encountered problems by overpricing their master franchise licenses in Europe. They rarely have completed market research to indicate the appeal of their product in another country, where it may be an unknown name and an untried system. Thus in essence, they are asking the master franchisee to spend its money to determine the product's appeal.

Internationally, each country has a limited amount of capital available from initial franchising fees. A $15,000 fee for each new unit may be more than the master franchisor is able to charge in the marketplace, which means that finding local franchisees can be a long, aggravating, and expensive process. What is sometimes overlooked is that expanding internationally will cost money before money comes back. If you decide to go international, it might be a year before you find somebody who wants to sit down and talk about taking a master franchise in another country. You need the right introductions to find people in the first place, and then there is no guarantee that the first person you meet will be the right person. And all the time you are spending money!

U.S. companies are becoming more realistic about making international franchises a long-term investment that emphasizes a steady stream of revenue rather than a large sum up front. It is advisable to meet with the franchisee and an accountant to create realistic projections of franchise openings over a five- to seven-year period, including how much the master franchisee might expect to earn as well as the amount you can legitimately take from the foreign operation. Franchise deals tend to collapse if the master franchisee is short on resources or does not take kindly to the franchisor's guidance. Warning signs of the master franchisee's shortcomings do come up. Unfortunately, businesspeople sometimes ignore these signals if they smell a deal.

Twenty years ago, a U.S. franchisor setting foot in Europe could be excused for ignoring warning signs or overlooking potential drawbacks to an international agreement. But the number of experienced business advisors and the wealth of literature available on the subject today mean that you can be much more prudent in your global franchising decisions. The Eastern Europeans in particular see franchising as a valuable business practice but, yet again, money is an issue. The development of indigenous franchises of the magnitude and level of those in comparable-sized western countries will take a lot longer in Eastern Europe because of the difficulty of raising money. Franchising is about expanding using other people's money. The rate of expansion in a country is limited by the availability of that money and the existence of reliable staffing to manage and run it.[8]

The following are some guidelines for considering franchising in foreign markets:

- You must do research in terms of the country's demographics, net disposable income, infrastructure (communications, transportation, education, etc.), tastes, preferences, and cultural mores to ensure that your franchise will work in that country.
- You may have to adjust your entry-level franchise fee to the country. Do not assume that demand for your franchise will be equally as strong as it is at home; it may take a while for the concept to take hold in foreign markets.
- You will probably have to adjust your product mix to the culture of the country (e.g., fast food in India cannot include beef products).
- You may wish to hire a local consultant or agent to represent you in your business negotiations in the foreign country. The cost of the local representative or agent could save you significant sums of money well into the franchise venture.

- Make sure that you allow for local advertising and promotion to reflect the culture of the country. Do not plan to export your domestic promotions, as they will most likely not work in the foreign country.

Strategic Alliances

Strategic alliances allow you to gain a foothold in a foreign country with minimal investment. They range from a handshake to a formal agreement between two parties. In simplest terms, a strategic alliance is an alliance with a partner, or a firm, in a foreign country that can act as your supplier, distributor, trading partner, local representative, and so on. This relationship can evolve over years of doing business together. Some advantages of strategic alliances are:

- Minimal cost of investment and maintenance of the relationship
- Ease of discontinuing the relationship
- Ability to form alliances with other partners, even competitors in foreign markets
- Ability to form local, global, regional, or multicountry alliances

Some disadvantages of strategic alliances are:

- Lack of control over copyright, patent infringement, and distribution channels
- Lack of control over local marketing and manufacturing
- Lack of control over competitors' signing similar agreements with the same partners

In spite of the disadvantages, most small businesses seek strategic alliances to minimize their up-front investment in foreign markets and to minimize the risk of entering these markets. Strategic alliances are only as good as the intentions of both parties. These relationships must be nurtured and must build trust to be successful in the long term. Although strategic alliances can be consummated with a handshake, it is wise to have a local representative in the country who can interpret the nuances and expectations of the agreement.

Overseas Joint Ventures

Overseas joint ventures are the next least-risky ventures in foreign countries. For small to midsize firms, an overseas joint-venture agreement may consist of the following:

- Identification of the appropriate local joint-venture partner, which has the labor force, local market, technology, or some other advantage for your firm
- Commitment of some capital, technology, management expertise, brands (marketing expertise), and so on to develop a local business in that country
- Negotiations involving a marketing relationship, manufacturing partnership, or technology-licensing venture
- Negotiations to determine how you will realize a profit out of the deal (this could be a challenge, particularly in emerging countries, such as China, where most of the comanufactured goods are exported to foreign markets as opposed to sold domestically)

A joint venture is a venture in the true sense of the word; there is no guarantee that both parties will achieve their business objectives. If, however, a joint venture does not provide a perceived benefit to both parties within a certain time frame, it is usually terminated. The following are some of the advantages of joint ventures:

- Relatively moderate investment of capital in terms of corporate funds, human capital, and so on, though at least a moderate amount of commitment must be made to make the venture work
- Agreements can usually be terminated on the basis of nonperformance, adverse market conditions, and even change of corporate direction
- Less risky than financing subsidiaries or an acquisition in a foreign country

Some of the disadvantages of international joint ventures are:

- Lack of control of management of the joint venture
- Lack of control of distribution of products or copyright or patent infringement

- Lack of ability to repatriate profits if most of the goods coproduced are for export (so although your risk is less with a foreign joint venture, your profit stream may be smaller, too)

Joint ventures exist in just about every country and region of the world. For success in foreign joint ventures, you need to take the following critical steps:

- Hire a skilled and loyal local representative to represent your firm in the negotiations. Provide enough incentives to ensure that this person brings a high level of commitment to the venture.
- Locate skilled, local management for the joint venture. If you hire an expatriate, make sure the person knows the local culture.
- Visit the country and your partners frequently. Lack of face-to-face involvement will result in failure of the venture.
- Lengthen your time frame for measurement of the venture's success (sales, market share, profits, etc.), as you are not dealing in your domestic market and you are assuming economic, political, and market risk factors.
- Make sure that you have a reliable source of local business intelligence. Frequently, joint-venture partners have trouble finding out what is really going on in the country.
- Have a reliable method (source) for tracking the distribution of your products, copyrights, or patents.

Overseas Subsidiaries

Overseas subsidiaries are a more structured option for international expansion in which the firm makes an investment in a local office, personnel, and manufacturing and marketing facilities. You may want to establish a local subsidiary in a foreign country for the following reasons:

- You already have a significant number of local customers, who need customer service and sales support. In this situation, the local office will be supported by the local sales production or distribution.
- You want control over your product distribution and, as much as possible, over copyrights and patents.
- You want to staff your local office with expatriates or locally trained staff.

- You want to control the local marketing, advertising, and promotion of your products.

For small to midsize firms just starting out in the international arena, the establishment of an overseas subsidiary may have the following disadvantages:

- High cost of incorporation in the local country (e.g., legal fees)
- Confinement of local labor laws
- Lack of developed infrastructure within the developing or emerging country

Small to midsize firms generally wait until they have achieved a certain volume of customers and sales in the local country before they establish a local subsidiary.

Overseas Acquisitions

Often it makes more sense strategically and economically to acquire a local firm rather than to reinvent the wheel or export products that would have to undergo considerable adaptation for the local culture. With international acquisitions, your due diligence must be five times greater than your due diligence for domestic acquisitions. If you are considering acquiring an overseas firm, you must address several key issues:

- It may be difficult to obtain accurate financial information on the firm you wish to acquire. Although you may have numbers, the accounting methods may differ significantly from your own, or the firm may have several sets of books, which may be perfectly acceptable in its country. You'll need to locate a reputable international accounting firm to perform this due diligence for you.
- You will have to conduct customer and marketing research on the company. You may think the firm has a major market position and satisfied customers, but this may not be the case.
- You will have to determine whether the local company can fit into your management style culturally. A mismatch in this area is one of the most common reasons for the failure of overseas acquisitions.
- You may want to consider the worst scenario. If the acquisition does not work, how much of a cash and emotional drain will your firm face?

Overseas acquisitions offer the acquiring company the following advantages:

- A successful and established market
- An established name and reputation
- An opportunity to leverage off this strength and develop new products from this base
- Quick start-up time to enter the local market

On the other hand, they present the following disadvantages:

- Relatively high cost
- Adherence to the local accounting methods, in addition to local taxation
- Difficulty finding someone to run the office

We have presented several options for going global. You will have to weigh the risk-reward trade-offs of these options and select the option that best fits the overall strategy of your firm.

CHAPTER
7

Global Selling

International business is driven by people and culture. Your firm may have the most advanced technology, product features, packaging, and the like, but if your international distributors or customers do not feel that you understand their culture, they will do business with others. In the dynamic, fast-paced global marketplace, understanding the regional and local culture of the country is the key to success or failure in the market.

Cultural Differences

In the United States—the "I" culture—people are driven by individuality; consumers, managers, and other individuals seek decision-making power and freedom of expression. In Asia, decisions are made in groups or by families; we could call this the "we" culture. Understanding various aspects of Asian cultures is critical in negotiations with their businesses. For instance, in Japan it is wise not to show emotions during negotiations, whereas in South Korea, displaying emotion over the terms of the deal is acceptable; harmony is central to the Chinese culture, and you should not show anger in dealings with the Chinese. Cultural awareness is also important to advertising in Asia. A competitive advertising campaign that defames your competitor's products would be a disaster there.

The European and Latin American cultures may be classified as the "they" cultures. Although diverse cultures occupy the same continent (e.g., French and German cultures in Europe, Portuguese and Spanish cultures in South America), each considers the others the "they" cultures. Thus a Pan-European or a Pan-Latin American marketing program is doomed to failure. The number one mistake made by small to midsize firms seeking global sales is to move ahead without a thorough understanding of the cultures in the foreign country. Understanding and empathy for the other culture is the decisive factor in strategic alliances, joint ventures, distribution agreements, customer negotiations, and so on. It is imperative for you to be well versed on diverse cultures and aware of the impact of myopic marketing thinking when entering foreign markets.

Chinese Culture

There is a parable of two companies, one U.S. and one French, that both badly wanted a $20 million contract to supply papermaking equipment in the People's Republic of China. During the business courtship, the U.S. executives received royal treatment from the executives in China and they returned the hospitality when their counterparts visited the United States. They proved their equipment was state-of-the-art and offered it at a competitive price that was within the Chinese budget. Yet, the French company ultimately won the contract, not because it offered a better deal, but because it made the Chinese executives feel more comfortable. The French executives listened more than they talked, and they didn't expect the Chinese to eat French food, for instance. These details are not trivial in the world of global business.

According to Mu Dan Ping, a partner in the Chinese Business Group at Ernst & Young LLP's Los Angeles office, business deals often fail not so much because of external factors—economics, technology, politics, and so on—but because of a lack of understanding between the two sides about cultural differences in personal values, perceptions, and expectations. If the French had lost the deal, it would have suggested that they should improve their papermaking technology. The Americans' losing, however, suggests that they should improve their cultural sensitivity— their relationship-building technology.

Like many immigrants to the United States, Mu struggled at first with the strangeness and unfamiliarity of things she didn't like or understand about life in her new country. She was locked in her own cultural prison, but when she changed her attitude, she started to enjoy life and to learn and grow. Mu believes Americans who go to China face a similar situation. They have to break through cultural barriers and reach out to understand things. We could argue that the Americans in our parable lost the deal through stupidity. We could also argue that the Chinese ultimately lost because they spent more money on inferior technology. According to Mu they lost because they based their decision on emotion. It's not that the Americans didn't respect the Chinese, but that the Americans did not know how to respect them in their own way.

When Chinese and Americans do business, both sides want to make a profit. What differs is their approach. If you can define the differences, you can find the common ground, compromise, and close the deal. Both cultures recognize the importance of hospitality, but define it differently (these differences are what soured the paper-mill deal). Americans often feel claustrophobic with the tight schedules arranged by their Chinese hosts. Busy American executives tend to consider sight-seeing and banquets a waste of time, whereas Chinese executives view these activities as providing opportunities to get to know one another before committing to business deals. Americans typically assume that their Chinese counterparts would like free time to shop and explore on their own when visiting the United States, but the Chinese may feel abandoned if left alone, even at their hotels. Chinese executives are put off by talking about business too soon. And despite the diversity of American cuisine, many Chinese have little appetite for non-Chinese food.

Whereas Americans separate their personal and professional lives, Chinese generally interact on a personal level, so aggressive negotiating behavior, or even political criticism, tends to be taken personally. In China, the bottom line is always, "Whom can I trust?" According to Mu, Americans mistakenly go to China looking for successful projects; instead, they should look for people who can successfully implement the projects. "They look for ways to make money in China, rather than looking for ways to work with Chinese."

American executives look for the rationale first. Is there a market with profit potential? If so, they want a contract before they waste time on a relationship. For Chinese executives, the priority is on the relationship. Once trust is established, they look for common goals. The contract serves to ensure mutual understanding rather than to provide recourse when disagreement occurs. The Chinese have a saying: "If you know yourself, you are intelligent. If you know others, you are wise." In other words, you have to learn what the other side wants. Gaining this knowledge requires constant and thorough communication, and in the end, if what the other side wants does not match your goals, says Mu, "You can walk away because you don't share the same vision."[1]

In cultivating business relationships in China, keep in mind the importance of hosting Chinese visitors and delegations in your home country. Prior to engaging in any business negotiations or making a business trip to the country, be sure to be briefed on local cultural issues. You may wish to hire a representative locally, who can brief you prior to the meetings.

In business dealings in China remember the following cultural dos and don'ts.

Do:

- Research the market thoroughly before your trip. Make sure that you are not meeting with competitive firms or with firms that may have signed agreements with your competitors.
- Book meetings well in advance. Confirm appointments at least one week ahead of the meeting.
- Hold your meetings either at your contact's firm or in the conference room, lobby, coffee shop, or restaurant of a good hotel.
- Allow time in your schedule for banquets and sight-seeing.
- Be briefed on the cultural issues of the country (e.g., the Chinese, out of politeness, always leave some food on their plate).
- Have an interpreter attend your meeting. Although Mandarin is the common written language throughout China, there are many spoken dialects.
- Research currency issues before your trip. Buying Chinese currency can be easier than selling it, as the government discourages the amount of hard currency available through the currency-sway exchanges. Sellers of renminbi (RMB, People's currency) recoup roughly half their original hard-currency cost.
- Arrive on time for dinners and banquets and never begin to eat or drink before your host does.
- Attempt to use chopsticks at all meals. Several courses or serving dishes will be presented and will not be passed around. You may reach in front of another person to get at the dishes, but you should not reach for the food with the end of the chopsticks that you put in your mouth.
- Use names and titles appropriately. Chinese names consist of a family name, a generational name, and a given name. Some Chinese executives may have adopted an English first name if they conduct a lot of business with English-speaking people.
- Dress conservatively (dark suits for both men and women for business and conservative casual dress also).

- Follow up on all business meetings. This step is essential in this fast-paced business environment and shows your commitment. E-mail is becoming as popular as fax communication in China.
- Give a gift from your whole company to the whole Chinese group and present it to the group's leader. Gifts representing your firm or your local region are appropriate. Do not wrap gifts in white as white is the color for funerals.
- Recognize that although handshakes are common, some Chinese may nod or bow slightly.
- Bring business cards with a translation in Mandarin on the reverse side. Place a business card given to you on the table, not in your pocket or wallet, and do not write on it.
- Allow enough time to get to business meetings. Rental cars are not available but taxis are reasonable and safe. In such cities as Shanghai, the subway is an efficient way to travel, although the system is not yet fully developed.
- Bring the necessary power transformer and adapter plug, as well as adapters for telephone jacks, if you travel with personal computer. Check with your modem manufacturer about the legality of using your specific modem in China.
- Schedule at least one or two trips a year to develop business. As older people are respected, send an older rather than a younger representative from your firm. The Chinese are sensitive to protocol and you may insult them if you send a young person to negotiate a business deal.[2]

Don't:

- As a general rule, discuss business at meals.
- Use exaggerated facial gestures or expressions when speaking or touch people who don't know you well.
- Express anger if you are not satisfied with the way the business negotiations are going. An expression of anger will indicate a lack of control over the situation.

In addition to the cultural issues, you should keep abreast of political issues that can affect your global sales. The Chinese government still plays an important role in business, and although it is beginning to emphasize decentralization and reliance on market mechanisms, its efforts are inconsistent. In addition, there is sometimes an element of paranoia that affects decisions based on political considerations. For example, a British consulting firm located in Beijing collected information on the Chinese government. A short time thereafter, all its Chinese clients suddenly terminated their contracts. The company learned that the information it had collected was considered confidential by the Chinese government.

Other Asian Cultures

Generally, the Chinese value trust, relationships, family, and harmony in their lives, and executives invest a significant amount of time in business networking to enable them to judge the integrity of their business associates. Yet in some ways the Chinese culture (and language) found in the People's Republic of China may vary from that found in Taiwan, Hong Kong, Singapore, and so on. Business executives are different in Taiwan, for example, where there is a capitalist orientation. It is important to understand the specific cultural mores of each country and not to assume a Pan-Chinese market.

Likewise, you cannot assume a Pan-Asian market. The Japanese, Korean, Thai, Indonesian, Malaysian, and other Asian cultures differ greatly from one another. Each country has distinct cultural values and business practices. In Japan, business decisions are made in groups, and executives are expected not to show exaggerated expressions in a business meeting. On the other hand, in South Korea, executives are more direct and do show emotion or enthusiasm over their products. In a business meeting in Indonesia, the word *yes* or a related expression may actually mean no, because in this culture people do not indicate rejection of ideas or things.

The bottom line is, you must do your homework. Hire a local representative to assist you in business negotiations in these countries and market your products on a country-by-country basis. Many firms have failed by trying to market products similarly in different Asian countries. Local market research will enable you to avoid these marketing and sales risks or potential disasters.

Latin American Culture

With the implementation of several trade pacts in this region (e.g., NAFTA, Mercosur, the Andean Pact) a number of the Latin American economies have stabilized and grown in the 1990s. This region is particularly attractive for small to midsize firms because of its proximity to the United States. Yet the geographical closeness belies the cultural differences.

Historically, Latin America has been plagued with high inflation and economic and political instability. This situation has turned around so that the region now presents several attractive market-expansion opportunities, although the following factors remain:

- Poor distribution channels and services
- Corruption and crime
- Currency fluctuations and devaluations and high inflation (vis-à-vis the United States)
- Bureaucratic procedures
- Underdeveloped infrastructure

Market research and expert target marketing and segmentation within the region are especially important because of the large disparity between the rich and poor populations. As the markets are diverse, research must address individual countries and their political and economic environment, along with distribution channels. The Mercosur trade pact, which consists of Brazil, Argentina, Paraguay, Uruguay, and Chile, has created a market of 200 million people and a combined GDP of $1 trillion. As a result of recently stabilized economies, many Latin American countries are developing consumer economies. However, Latin American consumers differ from American consumers and it is important to understand how they differ.

Latin American cultural values include:

- Strong respect for family values and for the elderly
- Absence of individual empowerment
- A live-and-let-live attitude
- Conservatism stemming from the pervasiveness of the Catholic religion
- Appreciation of U.S. products, but not necessarily of U.S. values

When selling in Latin American countries, do:

- Understand and abide by the rules of the Latin American culture.
- Learn the unique culture of the country in which you are doing business. Brazilians are friendly and outgoing; they will gesture and

may engage in physical contact. On the other hand, Venezuelans may behave more conservatively.

- Conduct local market research (country by country) to ensure that you understand the local market (e.g., Portuguese is spoken in Brazil, but Spanish is spoken in the other Latin American countries).
- Rely on personal relationships and face-to-face meetings.
- Speak the language (Spanish or Portuguese) fluently or hire a local representative who speaks the language to negotiate for you.
- Make business appointments three to four weeks in advance. Avoid scheduling business transactions around Carnival, which precedes Ash Wednesday, the beginning of Lent.
- Allow for lengthy trips, including late dinners (dinners usually start late and end late), usually best scheduled at first-class hotels.
- Plan to make several trips to Latin America to complete contract negotiations. Latin Americans can be offended by direct, get-to-the-point business behavior.
- Allow your contacts to work at their own cultural pace rather than according to your schedule.
- Reach the decision maker. Very few contracts can be signed by other senior managers.
- Keep your market-entry strategy simple and your market-entry costs low to offset inflation and currency fluctuations.
- Enter the market early and develop and adhere to a long-term mentality and perspective. Demonstration of your long-term commitment to the country or region is essential.

Don't:

- Make a commitment to a Latin American country and subsequently exit the country or region. This can be disastrous. The Latin American business community and consumers have memories like elephants—they never forget.
- Bring up business at meals, unless your host does so at the end of the meal. Meals are intended to allow you to get to know each other as persons and as potential suppliers or partners.
- Discuss political issues if possible. (Try discussing sports—Latin Americans, especially Brazilians, are avid soccer enthusiasts.)

 Case Study
What Works at Home May Not Work in Brazil

Wal-Mart was unable to export its tried-and-true formula for success in the United States to Brazil when it entered the Brazilian market through a joint venture. Because Wal-Mart could not act as a major distribution force in Brazil, as it does in the United States, it started a price war, selling all products at least 5 percent below its competitors' lowest price. Enraged at the start of a price war that could damage long-term interests and local business relationships, many suppliers suspended product sales and changed their negotiation conditions. One supplier actually had someone go to a Wal-Mart and buy all its own products off the shelves!

Wal-Mart was not operating in the United States, where it has thousands of stores, strong leverage with suppliers, state-of-the-art technology, and a distribution system to guarantee low prices and timely delivery. Thus, even though it achieved almost twice the sales volume of equivalent stores in the United States, Wal-Mart suffered losses of $16 million in the first forty days of operation and $33 million for all of 1996. The lesson to be learned is that the size, power, and knowledge that a company possesses in its home market does not automatically transfer to another country. You must understand the local competition and business environment. Use of a local partner or agent is helpful.

Western Europe

It is somewhat more comfortable for small to midsize firms to sell to countries in Western Europe that have modern, well-developed economies and economic and political stability. These countries do have differences in language, currency, and culture, and hence vastly different markets. On the other hand, Western European countries have legal systems that protect patents and copyrights. Furthermore, since the formation of the EU, most business executives are bilingual and speak some English.

Again, there is no Pan-European market. You need to approach this region on a country-by-country basis, including learning the dos and don'ts of each culture.

Central and Eastern Europe

The countries of Central and Eastern Europe have an underdeveloped infrastructure, high political risk, high inflation rates, and corruption. Nonetheless, some small to midsize firms have found significant market opportunities in these countries (e.g., Poland, the Czech Republic, Slovakia, Russia, Ukraine), particularly in the areas of energy, telecommunications, utilities, construction, and other industries undergoing privatization. Typically, though, it is the large, multinational firms that have the capital and staying power to absorb the risk in these countries until they stabilize.

Middle East and South Africa

Both large and midsize firms have shied away from the Middle East because of the political instability of the region and its Islamic culture. Saudi Arabia, Egypt, Morocco, Turkey, Israel, and Jordan are the most stable countries in the region. The United Arab Emirates' free-trade zone has attracted a significant amount of investment during the past few years. Adherence to and respect of the Islamic religion and cultural values is essential for doing business in this region. Violation of laws and cultural mores can result in imprisonment.

Since the abolition of apartheid, South Africa has emerged as a new market opportunity for large and midsize firms. Again, it is important to have a local representative who knows the old laws and new laws and the changing political, social, and economic conditions.

Resources

If you have a limited budget, you can access cultural information about countries on the Internet through the National Technical Information Service (NTIS). For a more in-depth overview, *Kiss, Bow or Shake Hands,* by Terri Morrison, Wayne A. Conaway, and George A. Borden, Ph.D. (Adams Media Corporation, 1994), gives extensive country history, and social and cultural details, country by country. This is a must read for cultural dos and don'ts.

Marketing Successes and Failures: Global Gold—Panning for Profits in Foreign Markets by Ruth Stanat (AMACOM, 1998) provides a comprehensive regional and country-by-country overview of the market opportunities and successes and failures in over thirty countries. This book also contains a complete source directory, by country, on industry and company contacts that can assist you with your expansion effort in the country.

If your budget is larger, Berlitz has excellent language and cultural training courses.

Copyright and Patent Issues

Small to midsize firms run a greater risk in terms of patent and copyright protection than do large, multinational firms, which have significant capital for international litigation and internal legal staffs. If your company has a unique or proprietary product or technology, you run a risk in countries that do not adhere to patent and copyright laws. Even in countries that give lip service to these international trade laws, it is extremely difficult to prove infringement and to enforce any type of penalty. Most often, the penalty is the loss of your proprietary technology or market position. For example, a Spanish beverage producer opened a branch in Tianjin, a northern coastal city in the People's Republic of China. After several years, the branch had achieved an excellent sales record. To exploit the growing demand, many Chinese companies copied the Spanish product in concept, packaging, brand design, and flavor. The Spanish company filed suit in a Chinese court. The Chinese government took the side of the local producers, and after three years, the case is still pending.

In another instance, a Swiss company introduced the first wear-resistant watch in 1962; in 1979, the company entered the People's Republic of China with an aggressive advertising program. Because of its global expansion plans, the firm registered its watch patent in countries around the world, but not in China.

Under Chinese law, a company must obtain a patent before entering the Chinese market; otherwise it cannot assert patent rights. A Chinese company produced an imitation of the watch, registered it with the Chinese patent office, and sold it at a price five times lower than that of the Swiss watch. Although the Swiss Company won the case, on the grounds of its activities elsewhere, the Chinese company was nevertheless given the right to produce and sell its watches, thus driving the Swiss manufacturer from the market.

The People's Republic of China is not the only country in which numerous cases of patent and copyright infringement have been reported.

It is important for you to research these laws and the experiences of other small to midsize companies in each country. The country reports produced by the NTIS outline the laws within each country, but do not mention the infringement cases in these reports.

Selling Your Products Globally

There are many options for selling your products globally. Some are low risk and low cost. To get started, you need to take the following steps:

- Identifying foreign buyers
- Qualifying potential buyers or representatives
- Locating overseas distributors
- Advertising your products globally

Identifying Foreign Buyers

There are many avenues for finding potential foreign buyers for your products.

1. **Advertise in Trade Journals.** Many small businesses report that foreign buyers often find them. An ad placed in a trade journal or a listing in the Department of Commerce's *Commercial News USA* can yield many inquiries from abroad. *Commercial News USA,* a catalog magazine featuring U.S. products, is distributed to 125,000 business readers in over 140 countries around the world and to over 650,000 Economic Bulletin Board users in 18 countries. The fees vary with the size of the listing. Many U.S. companies have had great success locating buyers through this vehicle. According to Brenda Dandy, vice president of Maryland's Marine Enterprises, "When overseas buyers contacted us through the *Commercial News USA,* we were thrilled." Exports now represent 20 percent of the company's sales.

2. **Participate in Catalog and Video-Catalog Exhibitions.** Catalog and video-catalog exhibitions are a low-cost means for you to introduce your products to potential partners at major international trade shows without leaving the United States. For a small fee, the US&FCS officers in embassies will show your catalogs or videos to interested agents, distributors, and other potential buyers. Several private-sector publications also offer the opportunity to display your products in catalogs sent

abroad. A few such publications are Johnston International's *Export Magazine, The Journal of Commerce,* and the Thomas Publishing Company's *American Literature Review.*

3. Pursue Trade Leads. Rather than wait for potential foreign customers to contact you, you can search out foreign companies that are looking for the particular product you produce. Trade leads from international companies seeking to buy or represent U.S. products are gathered by US&FCS officers worldwide and distributed through the Department of Commerce's Economic Bulletin Board. There is a nominal annual fee and a connect-time charge.

These leads are also published daily in the *Journal of Commerce* under the heading "Trade Opportunities Program" and in other commercial news outlets.

The World Trade Centers (WTC) Network allows companies to advertise their products or services on an electronic bulletin board transmitted globally. The U.S. Department of Agriculture (USDA) Foreign Agricultural Service (FAS) disseminates trade leads for agricultural products collected by their eighty overseas offices. These leads may be accessed through the AgExport FAX polling system, the AgExport Trade Leads Bulletin, the *Journal of Commerce,* or several electronic bulletin boards.

4. Exhibit at Trade Shows. The Department of Commerce's Foreign Buyer Program certifies a certain number of U.S. trade shows each year. Foreign buyers are actively recruited by DOC commercial officers, and special services, such as meeting areas and translators, are provided to encourage and facilitate private business discussions. International trade shows are another excellent way to market your products abroad.

For many small U.S. businesses, going to a foreign trade show once is not enough. According to John Stollenwerk, president of Allen-Edmonds Shoe Corporation, "You have to hang in there. In the beginning, in many countries where we displayed our products at foreign trade shows, we saw no results. But gradually people began to take our product, American-made shoes, seriously. We market our shoes as the 'world's finest.' That is one way American companies can compete." At present, 12 percent of the Wisconsin-based company's sales are derived from exporting.

Through a certification program, the Department of Commerce also supports about eighty international fairs and exhibitions held in markets worldwide. U.S. exhibitors receive pre- and postevent assistance. The USDA FAS sponsors about fifteen major shows overseas each year.

5. Participate in Trade Missions. Public and private trade missions are often organized cooperatively by federal and state international trade agencies and trade associations. Arrangements are handled for you so that the process of meeting prospective partners or buyers is simplified. Matchmaker trade delegations are DOC-sponsored trade missions to select foreign markets. Your company is matched carefully with potential agents and distributors interested in your product.

Tennessee-based Shaffield Industries, a futon manufacturer, reaped excellent returns as a result of a 1991 Matchmaker trade mission to Asia. "I was especially surprised at the high level of appointments scheduled for us during the Matchmaker trade mission. Each was a true prospect," reports David Goff, controller for Shaffield Industries. As a result of the mission, his company negotiated the sale of three containers of its product to South Korea and two containers to Taipei.

It is important, for you to be properly prepared for the kinds of inquiries you might encounter on overseas trade missions. The Small Business Administration (SBA) offers premission training sessions through its district offices and the SCORE program. Your local SBA office will have a schedule of upcoming "How to Participate Profitably in Trade Missions" seminars.

6. Contact Multilateral Development Banks. In developing countries, large infrastructure projects are often funded by multilateral development banks, such as the World Bank, the African, Asian, and Inter-American Development Banks, and the European Bank for Reconstruction and Development. Multilateral development bank (MDB) projects often represent extensive opportunities for small U.S. businesses to compete for project work. The Department of Commerce estimates that MDB projects could amount to at least $15 billion in export contracts for U.S. businesses. One business that successfully entered the international marketplace by bidding on a World Bank project is DSI in Poestenkill, New York. "As a result of World Bank loans to the People's Republic of China, DSI received over $1 million in contracts for laboratory equipment," reports DSI president, Dave Ferguson. Exports now account for 60 to 70 percent of DSI's business.

Development bank projects can be an excellent way to start exporting. Many small U.S. exporters have benefited from large MDB projects through subcontracting awards from larger corporations. A list of MDBs is included in part 2 of the *Exporter's Directory.* From their Washington,

D.C., headquarters, many MDBs hold monthly seminars to acquaint businesses with the MDB procurement process. Additionally, the DOC's Office of Major Projects can be of assistance in identifying contracting and subcontracting opportunities.

7. Contribute Articles to Journals and Make Public-Speaking Engagements. Writing articles for magazines such as *World Trade* and other international or globally focused publications will automatically extend the global reach of your products. Speaking engagements at conferences and trade associations will allow you to present your products and technology and state your desire to expand your business globally.

8. Develop Strategic Alliances in Foreign Countries. Through your own travel, participation in trade missions, and industry contacts, you may form a partnership with a company in a foreign country that can lead to your market expansion in the country. Word of mouth and personal referral are very powerful international marketing tools. Even relatives and friends located in foreign countries can help in this effort.

9. Sell Globally over the Internet. With the explosion of the Internet, your web site, if designed and worded properly, should attract foreign interest and potential buyers of your products. Follow-up, however, is essential. If you receive an inquiry from a foreign source, you should promptly reply.

One useful tool is STAT-USA/Internet, which helps small companies with a limited sales staff sell their products internationally. Eric Boothe, president of Electric Enterprises Incorporated (EEI) in Scottsdale, Arizona, and his partner, Paul Zvesky, started a full-service export management company for the sole purpose of exporting recycled and environmental products to markets around the world. The company's main focus has been sales in Western Europe, Eastern Europe, and Asia. EEI is a small firm (two full-time and one part-time employee) that serves as the export department of several different recycling facilities and manufacturers of environmental products.

With a small staff and some of the world's most attractive markets up for grabs, EEI needed a helpful sales tool to find valuable sales leads and market information for its clients' products. According to Boothe, "The EBB (on STAT-USA/Internet) has become one of the best sources of sales leads and export information for our company." An example of the company's use of EBB is the contract it recently signed to provide one thousand tons per month of recycled plastic material to a German company. This plastic material will be exported to India, where it will be made into fibers and sold to carpet and clothing manufacturers throughout the world. With the completion of the contract, EEI will have exported twenty-four million pounds of recycled plastics to India; these plastics would otherwise end up in landfills around our country. The contract was a direct result of a trade lead from the EBB and will generate up to $5 million of business for EEI.

Qualifying Potential Buyers or Representatives

Once you locate a potential foreign buyer or representative, the next step is to qualify the company by reputation and financial position. First, you should obtain as much information as possible from the company itself, by asking the following questions:

- What is the company's history and what are the qualifications and backgrounds of the principal officers?
- Does the company have adequate trained personnel, facilities, and resources to devote to your business?
- What is its current sales volume?
- What is the size of its inventory?
- How will the company market your product (retail, wholesale, or direct) or how will it use it?
- Which territories or areas of the country does the company cover?
- Does the company have other U.S. or foreign clients? Are any of these clients your competitors?
- What types of customers does the company serve?
- Does it publish a catalog?
- What are the size, structure, and capabilities of its sales force?

In addition, you should obtain references from several of the company's current clients. When you have this background information and are comfortable about proceeding, the next step is to procure a credit report about the company's financial position. The DOC's World Trade Data Reports (WTDR), available from your local International Trade Administration office, are compiled by US&FCS officers. A WTDR can usually provide an in-depth profile of the company you are investigating.

Several other commercial services are available for qualifying potential partners, such as Dun & Bradstreet's Business Identification Service and Graydon reports. U.S. banks and their correspondent banks or branches overseas, and foreign banks located in the United States, can provide specific financial information on companies.

Locating Overseas Distributors

The following are low-cost and efficient methods of locating trade leads and potential distributors for your business:

- **The Trade Opportunities Program.** This program provides private and public trade leads that arrive daily from U.S. embassies abroad. These leads are printed in the *Journal of Commerce* and other private-sector newspapers and are also available through the Economic Bulletin Board.

- **The Commercial Service International Contacts List.** This list can be found on disk 2 of the NTDB (National Trade Data Base) and can be searched by product and country of interest. It provides name and contact information for over seventy thousand foreign agents, distributors, and importers interested in working with U.S. exporters.

- **Agent/Distributor Service.** This is a customized search on behalf of U.S. companies seeking foreign representation. U.S. commercial officers abroad conduct the search based on your specific requirements. The search takes sixty to ninety days and costs $250 per market. You can place an order for this service through your local Department of Commerce district office.

- **Gold Key Service.** This service is custom tailored for U.S. companies planning on visiting a foreign country. It combines orientation briefings, market research, introductions to potential partners, interpreter service for meetings, and assistance in developing a marketing strategy. Your local Department of Commerce district office can provide more information.

- **Matchmakers.** These industry-specific overseas sales-promotion trips are sponsored by the Department of Commerce and usually include visits to more than one country. Companies can run booths or provide promotional materials to advertise their products or services and participate in prearranged business appointments and meetings.

Advertising Your Products Globally

Several years ago the marketing and sales literature was abundant with the concept of global branding. But as multinational companies increased their global expansion efforts, they discovered that this concept was only a concept. Global branding does not work in reality. Although global branding may achieve manufacturing and advertising efficiencies, each country is so different that implementation of global branding most often does not work, even with commodity products. What does work is the approach taken by Japanese businesses:

- Ongoing monitoring of global and competitors' markets, country by country
- Taking a product, improving its quality, and customizing the product for the culture and needs of the country
- Developing a specific advertising and promotion campaign, country by country

To advertise globally, at the bare minimum, you should have your product literature translated into the local language. It is important to have several checks on your translation. One advertisement for a U.S. airline in Latin America that originally stated, "We fly you in leather," translated into Spanish meant "We fly you nude." You will also need advice about what types of graphics, gestures of models, and colors may be offensive in that country. For example, the American sign for "okay" is obscene in Latin America (specifically, Brazil). In Asia, red is a happy color and white symbolizes death. In Japan, ornate and high-quality packaging sells the product.

Finally, have business cards made up with English on one side and the local language on the other to demonstrate your commitment to sales in the country.

Dos and Don'ts of Global Selling

Do:

- Adopt a global mind-set (a can-do attitude)
- Appoint an international champion to lead the effort
- Thoroughly research the culture of your target region and countries
- Organize a sales team (of local distributors, representatives, and translators) to assist you in the process
- Adapt your product and advertising and promotional program to the specific country
- Thoroughly investigate potential international customers

- Utilize the low-cost services that are provided by the Department of Commerce
- Use various methods to promote your products globally

Don't:

- Set up international meetings or attend trade missions unless you are *prepared*
- Assume a Pan-Asian, European, or Latin American market
- Assume that you can launch a global branding or global advertising program without modifications by country
- Assume that you can use direct, word-for-word translations

The Simplest, Cheapest, and Fastest Way to Sell Your Products Globally

The simplest, cheapest, and fastest way to sell your products globally is to do the following:

Change the name of your business by adding the word International at the end of it.

You do not even have to incorporate a new business. Within the United States, you can have an attorney issue a DBA (does business as) form for filing in the state in which you are currently incorporated. Also, you can have stickers made up inexpensively at a local print shop to put in your stationery and literature until your old supply runs out.

You will find that this simple name change will change the way your domestic customers, suppliers, and distributors perceive your business. Globally, in different countries, potential customers will perceive you as an international firm, rather than as a firm dedicated to its local market. Try it, and see the results for yourself.

CHAPTER 8

Changes at Home

One of the key challenges faced by senior management and owners of small businesses is how to organize the company to market its products globally. Although this is a major issue for firms with limited human and financial resources, it should not be overwhelming. You can do this on some very limited resources, but first you must separate the myths from the realities of what you are facing.

Myths about going global include:

- You need to hire a staff of multilingual nationals to market your products and service your company.
- You need to hire a high-cost vice president of international affairs to expand your business.
- You need to put up offices abroad and substantially increase your overhead.
- You need to hire expensive international lawyers to advise your marketing effort.
- This is a part-time effort.
- This is something that can be accomplished in the short term.

The realities of going global are:

- You will have to commit either yourself (president or CEO) or an experienced, senior staff member in your company to be your international champion and expand the business globally.
- This effort must be communicated to your entire organization and adopted by all members of your management and administrative team; it requires full commitment.

- Your international champion will be on the road, traveling at least 50 percent of the time, and his or her domestic responsibilities must be assumed by someone else.
- You will have to commit several members of your administrative staff to service international orders and the business abroad.
- You will have to educate yourself and your staff on how to finance international exports.
- You will have to ensure that you have sufficient staff to continue to service your domestic business.

What is the impact of these myths and realities? For most small to midsize businesses, the greatest strains in taking the initial step to go global come from:

- Riding the international learning curve—getting it right
- Limited human resources in servicing the business
- Limited financial resources in continuing to expand the business globally

Many executives of small businesses experience too many global opportunities for their products and services and as a result, have difficulty focusing their globalization efforts. In other words, demand for your products and services from several countries and regions of the world may force you to select and prioritize your global sales efforts. Certainly as the cash flow from your expanded international revenues increases, you will be able to expand and service other countries and regions of the world.

Some of the pitfalls experienced by small businesses in the early stages of global expansion include:

- Experiencing demand (and orders) from too many regions or countries
- Inability to secure the financing required to service the business
- Inability to commit the internal staff and financial resources to conduct preliminary market research
- Insufficient production capacity to meet the international demand, putting strains on your domestic demand
- Lack of capital to engage the services of exporters, consultants, and legal advisors

Many small to midsize firms have successfully overcome these hurdles with a carefully planned and executed international program. Such a program—its philosophy and short- and long-term objectives—must come from the top, senior management, and it must be adopted throughout the organization, to the lowest levels of management. The following section describes such a plan.

Step-by-Step Approach for a Planned and Successful International Program

Step 1: Communicate your global expansion plan, its objectives, goals, time frame, and expected results, to the entire organization

There should be no threats to the domestic business.
There should be no secrets about the international business.

Step 2: Identify and appoint the individuals who will be responsible for the execution of the program

You must shift their domestic responsibilities to other people in
the organization.

Step 3: Allocate sufficient financial resources for the following:

International market research
Financing of exports
Travel
Advertising and promotion (including translation of sales
literature)
International communications
Hiring some consultants in the field

Step 4: Analyze the success or shortcomings of your first effort prior to jumping into another country or taking on another international customer

This will enable you to avoid making the same mistakes twice.
This will help you to allocate your human and financial
resources for your next international customer or project.

Step 5: Make sure that your international business and objectives are integrated into your company's overall strategic plan and budget

International business should not be an afterthought or icing
on the cake.

Many firms welcome international sales but do not provide the
same service to their international customers that they
provide to their domestic customers.

Step 6: Budget for product customization for different countries and regions of the world

This item must be included in your capital investment and
marketing plans and budgets.

Step 7: Budget for the servicing of your international business

You may have to allocate staff in your domestic office.

You may have to appoint or hire a representative in the
country.

Step 8: Carefully evaluate whether to hire or contract staff domestically or internationally

It is often better to rent services until you have sufficient profits
and cash flow to support additional staff.

International representatives must be local people who speak
the language, who know the local culture, and who have
experience with your industry and products.

Step 9: Include your international business as you do your domestic business in your executive compensation program

Avoid making these competitive programs.

Make sure that these programs are perceived as contributing to
the profitability of the whole company.

Step 10: Use the intelligence that you gather from your international markets and customer experiences to improve your domestic products and business

You may wish to integrate foreign or competitive technology in
your products.

Use this market intelligence in your program of expansion to
other countries.

Organizational Success Stories

The following are examples of small businesses that executed well-planned international expansion programs. In each case, the international business has grown successfully within the organizational structure of the domestic business.

 Case Study
Donlar Corporation

Donlar Corporation of Bedford Park, Illinois, was incorporated in 1990. It manufactures polyaspartates, a derivative of polyaspartic acid, a polymer isolated from seashells. Donlar took research on how oysters form their shells and on synthetic analogs to this process, funded by the National Oceanic and Atmospheric Administration, and translated it into a viable commercial process.

The company's initial application was in industrial water treatment, to control the formation of calcium carbonate in pipes used for industrial steam heating and cooling. This application was the basis for Donlar's first patent; the company has since filed a total of thirty patents.

Polyaspartic acid is now used in many industrial applications, such as in preparing superabsorbents (e.g., used in baby diapers), in formulating cosmetics and hair sprays, as a dispersant in paints and pigments, in adhesives, and as a dispersant in detergents. Four to six percent of every box of detergent consists of this polymer, which prevents dirt particles from reattaching themselves to clothing. Polyaspartates are biodegradable, nonhazardous, and nontoxic. Aspartic acid is a key raw material in making polyaspartates.

A few years ago, Donlar researchers discovered that polyaspartic acid could be used to increase the area occupied by plant roots and thereby enhance the uptake of nutrients—nitrogen, phosphorus, and potassium—resulting in increased yields. Agricultural applications were forecast to be several times larger than industrial applications, and as a result, Donlar was split into two divisions.

Approximately 90 percent of Donlar's sales are domestic, and 10 percent international. Donlar's first international customer was Germany, which used its product in deep coal mines. The United Kingdom uses Donlar's products in secondary oil recovery in the North Sea, where environmental contamination has become a critical issue. The Europeans are about five years ahead of the United States on environmental protection legislation and are requiring the replacement of existing toxic and nonbiodegradable products with environmentally friendly alternatives.

As a result of its initial successful experience in Germany, Donlar expects to increase sales in Europe significantly over the next five years and anticipates exponential sales growth with its agricultural products. Sales for 1998 were expected to reach $10 million, and Donlar anticipates that figure to triple in the following two to three years. The firm has forty-five employees and plans to hire thirty additional workers for a plant it is building in Peru, Illinois. Donlar Corporation received the President's Green Challenge Chemistry Award in July 1996 in recognition of the company's environmentally safe chemistry.

Sometimes international sales limp along for a while. Until you gain confidence that there is a sufficient market overseas for your products, you should hold off on international expansion efforts. The following case illustrates this point.

 Case Study
Powell Books

Powell Books, of Portland, Oregon, established in 1971, carries both new and used books in the same store. According to its president, this mixture has been very successful. Powell's flagship store occupies a full city block, with more than a million volumes. The company has six specialty stores, more than three hundred employees, and a multilingual staff, and it now ships worldwide.

In 1986, Powell Books began exporting books to the Philippines for use in English-language training programs and libraries. Exports limped along until the company gathered confidence in the amount of overseas interest in English-language materials. Powell Books then began to sell what it couldn't sell in the United States—secondhand *Readers' Digest* condensed books, old editions of technical books, and other materials of little value or interest to an American audience. The company moved materials into a variety of international markets with virtually no in-house expertise. With an interest but no time for competent sales follow-up, Powell Books hired an export manager in 1992 to handle the program.

How did Powell Books get started in globalizing its small business? It began by contacting the International Trade Administration for a list of Philippine companies that sold used books and writing those companies about the books Powell had to sell. Powell Books is still doing business with a company from that list, and the Philippines continues to be a regular market for Powell.

The company also regularly exports to Korea, which has become its largest market, and to the People's Republic of China (Guangzhou and Shanghai) and Vietnam. Powell Books was the first U.S. company to ship to Vietnam. Powell Books exports small shipments to Singapore and Japan and anticipates making sales in Malaysia soon. It exports small shipments to Brazil and to countries such as Bulgaria, Hungary, Poland, Estonia, and the Czech Republic in Eastern and Central Europe. Powell is exploring the possibility of exporting its books to Chile and to South Africa.

According to the company's export manager, the ITA helped it find buyers overseas and obtain a license, citing exemptions for printed matter. The ITA helped accelerate Powell's credibility in Asia, particularly in China and Vietnam, where only government agencies are allowed to import books.

According to Powell's president, there are some pretty hefty barriers to joint ventures in the industry. Books are inexpensive; shipping is expensive—that's the dynamics. Powell does about half a million in export sales. It's a small part of the business, which Powell plans to pursue aggressively. The company makes a lot of sales over the Internet, and visits overseas customers twice a year. Powell Books is satisfied with growth of 20 to 25 percent in exports each year.

These small businesses used the assistance of low-cost agencies and experienced success in one country or a region prior to expanding further internationally. Whereas the company president was the initial international champion, each firm subsequently hired someone or dedicated a resource to the international expansion effort.

What If You Miss an International Market Opportunity?

What happens if you discover that there is a trade exhibition, mission, or conference in a country and you have either missed the deadline or do not have time to prepare for the event? You can use this time to gather market research and information and make the market introduction at a later date. The following example illustrates how one company turned its missed opportunity into a success story.

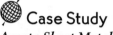 Case Study
Acosta Sheet Metal Manufacturing

Acosta Sheet Metal is a small manufacturer of sheet-metal products for residential, commercial, and architectural metal applications. It was founded by Sal Acosta in 1972. According to the company's general sales manager, Acosta Sheet Metal first became interested in exporting in October 1993 when it received a flyer from the Chamber of Commerce describing an upcoming Commerce Department trade delegation to Mexico City. The company thought this would be an excellent opportunity, but missed the deadline and was not selected. The company then learned of a delegation in April 1994 to Monterrey, Mexico. The six months' lead time gave Acosta the opportunity to discover what sells in Mexico, and the company used the time to send information and samples to potential customers.

When Acosta Sheet Metal went on the mission, all the people it had wanted to contact, plus others it hadn't expected, were there. The company met with numerous manufacturers. Acosta spent about a year getting to know the people and how they worked. It found it had to do a lot of educating, which generated more work for the organization. This planning process took a lot of time. Finally, Acosta selected one or two companies with which to do business in Mexico.

In short, Acosta Sheet Metal's missed opportunity enabled it to plan for its sales effort. The company made twenty-three contacts and ended up with five that were viable, that is, that had the resources and technology to manufacture what Acosta manufactured in the United States. Acosta exported some products prior to the devaluation of the peso; subsequently, the Mexican economy slowed, and the company began to manufacture its products in Mexico to be price competitive. Because Mexico and Chile have a free-trade agreement, Acosta could use some materials from Chile, which were less expensive.

Acosta Sheet Metal is expecting growth to be about 35 percent; it grew 10 percent in its first six months in Mexico. Acosta feels if it does a good job, the opportunities could be endless. It has been visited by a Mexican steel-producing firm, which has opened a new door of opportunity in promoting metal roofs in Mexico, as well as by a U.S. manufacturer of sealants. This manufacturer is also interested in manufacturing and selling its products in Mexico. All of these events have begun to trigger more business opportunities for Acosta. The missed opportunity that enabled Acosta to do its homework has resulted in a profitable extension of its domestic business.

How Should You Staff Your Overseas Operation?

Chapter 6 discussed your options for going global (exporting, joint ventures, strategic alliances, direct investment, etc.). Each of these options will have an impact on your company at home. Small businesses usually begin by exporting their products and services to international markets, as this approach carries less financial and market risk. Once your product or service is established in a country or a foreign market, you may need to add local customer service and support. The economics of the country (e.g., lower labor costs, abundant technical labor) may encourage you to manufacture your product there. On the other hand, although the economics may justify a formal joint venture or foreign direct investment, you may experience problems in the distribution of your products in the country (e.g., People's Republic of China, Chile) or the region (e.g., South America).

How do these issues affect your organization? Historically, most large, multinational firms gain entry into foreign markets through exports, obtain sizable market share, revenues, or profits, and then either invest directly in the country or enter into joint-venture agreements, which reduces their risk in the country. During the 1960s, '70s, and early '80s, management of these international operations (subsidiaries and so on) was staffed by people trained in the United States or by U.S. expatriates. The large multinationals have learned painfully over the past few decades that this approach does not work over the long term. These foreign operations need to be staffed and run by people from the country who know the local culture and market.

What are the implications of these staffing issues for a small business? To establish your company in a country, you may have to dedicate someone from your home office who can travel back and forth to the country or temporarily live in the country to implement the sale-and-distribution program or the manufacturing operation. If you enter into a strategic alliance with a foreign partner, it is unlikely that you will have to relocate someone to the country as most of the work can be done from the home office.

On the other hand, if you enter into a joint venture and are investing significant amounts of capital in the country, you will need someone from your home office or a local manager to oversee the joint venture. Absentee ownership or management does not work internationally. You must have a continuing presence to ensure the success of the venture.

Most small businesses that have achieved success in a foreign country or market find they need a local representative. This person does not have to be a current employee. Through your contacts in the country, you can appoint a local representative (from the local culture) to represent, service, or sell your products. However, as this person will represent your product, and hence your company, and can succeed or fail with the effort, you must take great care to select the right person. You will have to investigate whether the person represents competitors' products in the country or the region, as well as other potential conflicts of interest, which could damage your product's image. Frequent field visits and constant communication with your representative will be critical to your success in the country.

Other Organizational Issues

Do not think that expanding your business to a foreign country or globally will not have an impact on your organization. It most definitely will. The challenge is to make it a positive impact that enhances your domestic business, rather than a negative impact. The following are some of the positive changes within your organization that can occur as a result of global expansion:

- **Improved market intelligence or information about your local and international competitors' products, technology, strategy, production, and management techniques.** If you have a global presence, you are continually aware of competitive moves, prices, distribution plans, and so on. Your domestic business does not give you firsthand access to this local international information.

- **Increased market opportunities for your products and services.** If your products have reached maturity in your local market, you may be faced with having to reduce your production and administrative staff. Global expansion may keep these people employed and ensure the long-term viability of your business. Much of the growth of small businesses today is coming from international markets. Choosing not to participate in these markets puts your firm at a further disadvantage domestically.

- **Improved production, management, and technology.** Companies in some countries may have more efficient methods of production, improved technology, and access to more human and capital resources. Knowledge of and access to these methods can allow you to import them back to your domestic market.

- **Better employee morale and ability to attract high-quality labor.** Small to midsize firms that are international have a better chance of attracting higher-quality and more-skilled labor. Young and educated workers seek careers in firms that offer opportunities to grow and expand their skills.

- **Increased domestic business.** Companies in your home country may learn that you are international or are doing business in a particular country or region and may contact you for additional business. They may want to distribute their products through your firm or perhaps co-market their products with yours.

- **Stabilized customer base.** International customers are for the long term. If they have a consistent and high-quality supplier, they are generally more stable than are domestic customers, who leave for a percentage difference in price.

The following are some of the negative impacts that going global might have on your organization:

- **Strain on organizational resources.** At least in the short term, international prospecting and export orders can strain the human and financial resources of your organization. This situation may persist until the revenue and profit stream from international sales can support hiring additional staff dedicated to the international effort.

- **Disruption of your domestic business.** International orders may cause disruption to your domestic production cycles, quality-control procedures, and sales organization.

- **Increased financial pressures.** Taking international orders will increase financing and cash-flow pressures. Thus it is important to utilize the low-cost governmental programs that are available.

- **Longer time frame for delivery of results.** If your company is publicly held and pressured for short-term profits and performance, international expansion can create a severe strain, as it necessarily lengthens the time frame for delivery of results. International expansion is a long-term process with long-term results. Your shareholders may not understand or have the patience to yield gains in foreign markets.

Most small to midsize businesses generally experience more positive impacts than negative impacts from their international expansion efforts. Firms that experience difficulties with international expansion usually either drop the initiative or choose to enter the markets at a later date when their organization will be better able to handle these issues.

Some global markets or countries may have to mature before they will be ready for your products. This situation occurs most frequently for high-tech products, consumer products, and entertainment products. Developing and emerging-growth countries need to have basic infrastructures (transportation, health-care, communication, educational systems) in place before they are ready for the introduction of more sophisticated goods and services. This situation should not preclude market intelligence monitoring efforts to keep you abreast of potential emerging opportunities. Even more than for large, multinational firms, early market entry is critical for small to midsize firms, which do not have the capital and human resource base to ward off competition. Your company needs to capitalize on its product uniqueness and timing in the foreign market.

Make a list of the positive and negative impacts that global expansion could have on your business. If positive impacts outweigh negative, as in the following case study, you should be ready to begin the process of global expansion.

 Case Study
Applied Science Associates, Incorporated

Applied Science Associates, Incorporated (ASA), Narragansett, Rhode Island, is a privately held, multidisciplinary environmental consulting firm specializing in the development and application of computerized tools to investigate complex environmental and engineering issues in fresh and marine waters. Founded in 1979, ASA develops computer models to predict where spilled hazardous materials, particularly oil and chemicals, will travel and to assess damages, hydrodynamics, impact on water quality from discharge, and related environmental problems. ASA evolved from funding for a program called Sea Grant, which created an environment in which research work in developing coastal circulation and pollutant-transport modeling could proceed.

According to Dr. Malcolm Spaulding, founder, former president, and current adviser to the firm, ASA has just sold a model to the National Institute of Ocean Technology in Madras, India, which is looking at the impact of port and harbor development on water quality. ASA is working with the Omanis on coastal circulation and has provided oil-spill modeling assistance in the South China Sea and for Vietnam. Australia has adopted one of ASA's models as its national standard for oil-spill modeling. The company is also assisting Indonesia and Thailand on water-quality problems resulting from rapid development.

This company carefully weighed the positive and negative impacts of going global on its business. The competition in the business is incredibly fierce. ASA now operates in a global competitive arena, rather than a local market. Much of the international competition comes from large, European government laboratories that have been privatized and are still subsidized. Because each European country has developed a lab to perform this kind of work, there is only modest demand for ASA's services in Europe now. The principal growth and problems are in the developing countries.

According to ASA management, "If you don't keep growing, you'll die." Revenues are currently about $1.3 million a year, although they have been as high as $2.4 million. The company views international growth as a means to reach its former revenue level. To augment the international effort, it is developing new products. The COAST MAP, an integration of modeling and monitoring, was developed as a part of a teaming arrangement with an equipment manufacturer. The equipment manufacturer didn't want to develop software and ASA had no interest in developing hardware; the arrangement allowed the companies to develop a product together that neither would have been able to develop alone. This result was a logical evolution of ASA's business.

ASA was faced with declining domestic growth and increased global competition. Its decision to expand globally was a matter of the future long-term health of the business.

Impact of Going Global on Human Resource Requirements

Most small to midsize businesses have to expand their sales and marketing resources to meet the needs of their global customers. Usually the effort is driven by the CEO, president, or international champion and supported by the vice president of sales or sales manager. As your export orders increase, you may need to add customer-service support staff, preferably people who speak the local language of your international customers. With expanded international operations, you may have to put an existing sales staff member directly in charge of export sales or hire an experienced person from outside the firm. When international sales become a significant percentage of your overall revenues, you will be faced with the issue of whether to organize a separate international department or an international staff within each of your company's divisions, lines of business, or product lines.

The approach you should take depends on the culture of your firm. If your firm is organized by functional areas (manufacturing, sales, finance, etc.), then it makes sense to organize a separate international department. With this approach, the international coordination effort will be consistent, but the staff may not be technically conversant in all product lines and details of the technology.

On the other hand, if your firm is organized and run according to separate business units, operating divisions, or product lines (with separate profit centers), it may make sense to organize your international staff within these units so staff members can focus on the global expansion of their particular products. If you take this approach, you also need to take steps to ensure that there is a coordinated international effort among the various business units, operating divisions, or product lines. Otherwise, you risk:

- Duplication of sales effort in a country
- Lack of coordination of sales efforts
- Confusion in the local marketplace
- Inability to leverage internal resources

International business evolves over a period of time, and your organization should adjust to the changes. For most small to midsize firms this evolution is positive and contributes to the long-term health of the firm.

CHAPTER

9

Measuring Your Success

The secret of all good marketing is monitoring progress and the level of success. This process permits the constant reshaping and fine-tuning needed to convert investment in global marketing into profits and to keep the profits growing. It would be truly amazing if progress in the global market proceeded in accordance with the initial global marketing plan. The process is a learning experience, and the activities, time scales, and costs defined on the basis of an analysis of the global opportunity will inevitably need to be modified in the light of experience. Often plans are overly optimistic, and objectives need to be diluted as progress turns out to be slower than forecast. Less frequently, analysis underestimates the potential of global markets and plans need to be revised upward. The key requirement for success is to remain flexible and review progress at regular intervals.

Most companies measure their progress in all their activities in light of what is happening to the bottom line. Profits, or progress toward profits, equal success; losses equal failure. There is nothing wrong with this measure; at the end of the day, the contribution of the global marketing program to bottom-line performance is what really matters. However, in marketing, financial measurements are rarely enough, because they tend to record only what has already happened, or what is expected to happen in the short-term future, whereas marketing is more concerned with the middle- and long-term future.

Any measurement of success in marketing needs to consider several parameters, which have both a direct and an indirect connection to the bottom line. Most of these are covered in the global marketing plan which should cover:

- Global sales projections
- Market-share analysis
- Efficiency of the marketing program
- Effectiveness of the marketing program
- Reasons for lost business
- Distributor and customer satisfaction
- Development of the global-marketing skill base
- Staff satisfaction

Global Sales Projections

The record of global sales broken down by country and customer type is the basic yardstick of performance and success, and comparisons with budgeted sales show the extent to which reality is keeping pace with the plan. It would be truly surprising if actual sales followed the plan perfectly—too many variables are outside the control of the company. Nevertheless, variances should be positive as well as negative and over time a general pattern should emerge, which may suggest changes in the intensity and direction of the marketing effort. If all the variances are heavily adverse, your company should have growing doubts about whether the program can be sustained, either in specific countries or in the global market as a whole.

Information on global sales should include projections of where sales are heading, based on experience and statements or feelings coming back from the marketplace. Beware of hockey-stick projections, which have a flat historical profile and soar like an eagle beyond some date in the immediate future. These defy credibility unless there are some strongly documented reasons for the pattern of sales in the future to depart radically from the pattern that has prevailed in the past.

It is advisable to set up a formal program of monthly and quarterly reports from each territory covering the key elements of performance, including:

- Sales in the period
- Comparisons with budget
- Reasons for variances
- Sales projections for the remainder of the year

- Longer-term outlook
- Current trading conditions within the market
- Trading outlook

The reporting format has to be relatively simple or the reports will not be completed. You can, however, ask for periodic additions, such as a three-year outlook, to assist the budgeting process. The main problem with these reports is that, like most sales reports, they are likely to be completed by individuals who are not equipped to take an objective view of the future. Depending on your market-entry method, they may or may not be employees of your company. If they are not, you may not be able to rely on the data. Agents, distributors, or licensees are likely to want to prolong a business of interest to them, even if it is not important for you. Sometimes cultural reasons prevent a person from making any admission of failure. Therefore, the data should be examined carefully and verified independently, preferably by your own staff.

There is no point in collecting information unless you are going to use it. You'll need a central person responsible for collecting the information, verifying it, assembling it into an analysis of the global situation, drawing conclusions, and distributing it.

Market-Share Analysis

Market share is another primary indicator of success because it measures the impact of your company relative to other suppliers in the market. Market share can be calculated for the market as a whole, but it is more useful to look at shares within the specific segments of the market that you are targeting. In some cases, microscopic market shares generate large revenues and may therefore be perfectly acceptable, but in many markets the achievement of a significant market share is essential for survival.

A low market share may be a direct consequence of inadequate performance (i.e., unsuitable product, poor distribution, or poor marketing), but it can also indicate that the competitive reaction to your market entry has been so strong that your company is struggling. Whatever the cause, low market share argues for improvement and intensification of the marketing effort, assuming that it can be justified in terms of the additional sales that will be generated.

The calculation of market share requires data on total sales in the market and sales within each market segment. To collect this information, the market-research effort must be updated at regular intervals. This process is easiest for consumer goods markets, for which tracking data are available in most countries; it is most difficult for specialist industrial markets.

Efficiency of the Marketing Program

Efficiency can be measured by calculating the volume of sales generated by each marketing dollar. This measurement can highlight differences between the home market and each global territory. Global marketing costs can be inherently higher than domestic costs, particularly in the early years, but less so once your company has become an established global supplier. The early stages of global development require substantial marketing investments in travel, staff time, and other expenses while your company is building its position. However, local marketing costs can vary significantly from country to country, and in some countries may be significantly lower than they are at home, thus offsetting the higher central costs.

Effectiveness of the Marketing Program

Marketing efficiency is also a reflection of the effectiveness of your marketing program in creating sufficient awareness of your product or service and in winning business. Effectiveness depends on choosing the right marketing methods and using the right marketing messages. As we have shown, surveys can be used to determine awareness levels, the image held of the supplier, recall of the marketing techniques used, and the extent to which potential customers remember the marketing messages that have been used. High levels of awareness and marketing-message recall usually mean that the marketing program has reached its target audience. However, recall does not pay bills, and there is no point in winning awards for marketing activities that do not generate enough sales.

Specific measurements of effectiveness you should consider are:

- Sales per personal salesperson or per telemarketing salesperson
- Readership of newspapers and journals carrying company advertisements

- Recall of the messages contained in company advertisements
- Comparative performance of major competitors
- Take-up rates on promotions
- Attendance at exhibitions at which your company promotes its products
- Visitors to company stands
- Column inches resulting from company PR
- Distributor shelf space devoted to your products

The benchmarks against which these measurements should be compared are the performance figures for your home market.

Reasons for Lost Business

In marketing you can learn as much—or more—from mistakes as from successes. Studying the reasons for lost business is a useful supplement to other forms of analysis and may point to possible changes in the marketing program. Data can be collected informally by following up whenever significant orders are lost. Those handling the follow-up must take care to get beyond superficial and face-saving responses, however. For instance, price is commonly given as the reason for not placing an order even when it is not the determining factor.

It is also important to review the circumstances when merchandise is returned or orders are canceled before being fully completed. These situations occur when there is a perceived failure in the product or level of service. The situation is especially serious if the problem does not lie with the product or service itself, but in the product's failure to live up to the expectations raised by the marketing program.

Distributor and Customer Satisfaction

The extent to which you meet the expectations of your global distributors and final customers is a primary indicator of success and will have a profound impact on your future business. If you generate high levels of customer satisfaction, particularly in the early days of your global marketing efforts, you will be well placed to succeed in the future—as long as you continue to make a profit. High levels of customer satisfaction have a multiplier effect in that satisfied customers make repeat purchases and can recommend suppliers to their friends and business colleagues. The reverse is equally true; it has been estimated that each dissatisfied customer recounts that dissatisfaction to an average of twelve others.

Customer satisfaction has added importance in global markets, where the interactions among product, service, and customer are less predictable than in the home market. However well the market is tested, only the real experience of selling to customers will reveal whether the complex chemistry that exists in the market will work to your advantage.

Customer-satisfaction surveys can be used to monitor your company's performance at regular intervals. Unfortunately, surveys are usually expensive, largely because they need to be based on a representative sample of customers or distributors and, to avoid bias, should be carried out by an independent agency. They are well worth the expenditure, however. It is no accident that a high proportion of *Fortune* 500 suppliers rely on the results of customer-satisfaction surveys as a measure of their performance; some even base the bonuses of their executives on the findings.

Development of the Global Marketing Skill Base

The rate at which the global marketing skill base improves is a more subjective measurement of performance. Most companies are novices when they commence their global marketing programs, but the hard school of experience improves their skills over time. Regular skill audits will show the extent to which skills are improving and highlight areas of deficiency that need to be addressed.

Staff Satisfaction

The final measure of whether it is all worthwhile is staff satisfaction. The staff involved in the global marketing effort need to understand the objectives of the program, be comfortable with the approaches being used, and be sufficiently motivated to continue with it. Nothing kills a marketing program more quickly than demoralized or demotivated staff, and the personal attractions of global marketing—foreign travel, new challenges, and duty-free liquor—soon appear superficial if the task itself is perceived as unrewarding.

To promote staff satisfaction your company can initiate a program of frequent discussions to review personal and company progress and to identify methods of improving performance by taking account of the opinions of those on the front line. The program should include partners active within the global territories. They can offer firsthand opinions of whether your global marketing effort is as successful as it could be and what changes might result in improvements. Consulting people lets them buy into the marketing program and provides them with an incentive to make sure it works. And making it work is what this is all about.

The Future

As we enter the next century, small to midsize businesses will make the world their oyster. Most firms will recognize that they will have to compete in a global marketplace to survive, and most will become larger players in the global arena through strategic partnerships and alliances throughout the world. Firms that have a stake in the global marketplace or have achieved global equity—having a successful presence in two or more regions of the world—will have a higher probability of surviving in the future. Small to midsize firms can begin to plan for the future by taking advantage of the opportunities that await them throughout the world.

In some respects, the question is not whether to go global, but when to go global. Only the owner or the chief executive of a firm can address this issue. As you enter the next millennium, you want to be sure that you do not carry forth global blind spots that can leave your firm at a competitive disadvantage in the global marketplace. To this end, *Global Jumpstart* will help you well into the future.

Appendix I: Five Stages of Organizational Development for Small Firms*

*Adapted and reprinted by permission of *Harvard Business Review.* From "The Five Stages of Small Business Growth," by Neil C. Churchill and Virginia L. Lewis, May–June 1983. Copyright 1983 by President and Fellows of Harvard College; all rights reserved.

FIVE STAGES OF ORGANIZATIONAL DEVELOPMENT FOR SMALL FIRMS

STAGE	MAIN PROBLEM/QUESTIONS	MANAGEMENT FACTORS				
		MANAGEMENT STYLE	ORGANIZATIONAL STRUCTURE	FORMAL SYSTEMS	MAJOR STRATEGIC GOALS	OWNER'S INVOLVEMENT
Existence	Obtaining customers 1. Can we get enough customers, deliver our products, and provide services well enough to become a viable business? 2. Can we expand from that one key customer or pilot production process to a much broader base?	Directly supervises subordinates who should be of at least average competence.	Simple.	Systems and formal planning are minimal to nonexistent.	Remain alive.	Does everything. Performs all the important tasks, and is the major supplier of energy, direction and, with relatives and friends, capital.
Survival	Business is workable as a business entity. Has enough customers and satisfies them sufficiently. Key problems shift to the relationship	Limited number of employees supervised by	Simple, but instead carries out the rather well-defined		The major goal is still survival.	Owner still synonymous with the business.

Survival (continued) | between revenues and expenses. Key issues are:

1. In the short run, can we generate enough cash to break even and to cover the repair or replacement of our capital assets as they wear out?

2. Can we, at a minimum, generate enough cash flow to stay in business and to finance growth to a size that is sufficiently large, given our industry and market niche, and make an economic return on our assets and labor?

a sales manager or general foreman. Neither of them makes major decisions.

orders of the owner.

STAGE	MAIN PROBLEM/QUESTIONS	MANAGEMENT FACTORS			
		MANAGEMENT STYLE	ORGANIZATIONAL STRUCTURE	FORMAL SYSTEMS	MAJOR STRATEGIC GOALS	OWNER'S INVOLVEMENT
Survival (continued)	Stays in survival, gaining marginal returns, and dies when owner gives up or goes onto the next stage if it has developed economic viability.				
Success— disengagement	Decision is whether to exploit the company's accomplishments and expand or keep the company stable and profitable, providing a base for alternative owner activities. The company attains true economic health, has sufficient size and product-market penetration to ensure economic success, and earns average or above-average profits.	Requires functional managers to take over certain duties performed by the owner.	Cash is plentiful; the main concern is to avoid a cash drain in prosperous periods to the detriment of the company's ability to withstand inevitable rough times. First professional staff members enter (controller, production scheduler).	Planning in the form of operational budgets supports function delegation.	The owner, and to a lesser extent, the company's managers, should be monitoring a strategy to essentially maintain the status quo.	As the business matures, it and the owner increasingly move apart, partly because of the owner's activities elsewhere and partly because of the presence of other managers.

The company can stay in this stage indefinitely, provided environmental changes do not destroy its market niche or ineffective management reduces its competitive abilities.

Issue: Whether to use the company as a platform for growth or as a means of support for the owners as they completely or partially disengage from the company.

The managers should be competent but need not be of the highest caliber, since their upward potential is limited by the corporate cash goals.

Basic financial, marketing, and production systems are in place.

The owner and, to a lesser extent, the company's managers, should be monitoring a strategy. This is essential to maintain the status quo.

Additional goals vary depending on the owner's desire to sell, accrue, or grow.

Behind the disengagement might be a wish to start up new enterprises, run for political office, or simply pursue hobbies and other outside interests while maintaining the business more or less in a status quo.

		MANAGEMENT FACTORS				
STAGE	MAIN PROBLEM/QUESTIONS	MANAGEMENT STYLE	ORGANIZATIONAL STRUCTURE	FORMAL SYSTEMS	MAJOR STRATEGIC GOALS	OWNER'S INVOLVEMENT
Success— growth	Owner consolidates the company and marshals resources for growth. The owner takes the cash and the established borrowing power of the company and risks it all in financing growth.	Shift from current to future orientation and moves toward strategic planning. Improving systems and control and delegation. Need for quality and diversity.	Hiring managers with an eye to the company's future rather than its current condition.	Systems should be installed with attention to forthcoming needs. Operational planning is in the form of budgets, but strategic planning is extensive and deeply involves the owner.	Making sure the basic business stays profitable so that it will not out-run its source of cash, and developing managers to meet the needs of the growing business. Hiring managers with an eye to the company's	The owner is much more active in all phases of the company's affairs than in the disengagement aspect of this phase. If successful, it moves into the next stage; if not, it may cause retrenchment to survival state, prior to bankruptcy or distress sale.

FIVE STAGES OF ORGANIZATIONAL DEVELOPMENT FOR SMALL FIRMS (cont.)

Success—growth (continued)					future rather than its current condition.	
Takeoff	How to grow rapidly and how to finance that growth. The most important questions are: 1. Can the owner delegate responsibility to others to improve the managerial effectiveness? Will the actions be true delegations with controls on performance and a willingness to see mistakes made, or will it be abdication? 2. Will there be enough cash to satisfy the great demands growth often brings (will the owner tolerate a high debt—equity ratio) and a cash flow that is not eroded by inadequate expense controls or ill-advised investments brought about by owner impatience.	Key managers must be very competent to handle a growing and complex business environment.	Decentralized and, at least in part, divisionalized (usually sales or production).	Strained by growth, are becoming more refined and extensive. Both operational and strategic planning are being done and involve specific managers.	Balance growth with finance. Develop better management strategies, often decentralization creating divisions to improve organizational and strategic planning.	Owner and the business have become reasonably separate, yet the company is still dominated by both the owner's presence and stock control.

FIVE STAGES OF ORGANIZATIONAL DEVELOPMENT FOR SMALL FIRMS (cont.)

STAGE	MAIN PROBLEM/QUESTIONS	MANAGEMENT FACTORS				OWNER'S INVOLVEMENT
		MANAGEMENT STYLE	ORGANIZATIONAL STRUCTURE	FORMAL SYSTEMS	MAJOR STRATEGIC GOALS	
Takeoff (continued)	Questions: 1. Do I have the quality and diversity of people needed to manage a growing company? 2. Do I have now, or will I have shortly, the systems in place to handle the needs of a larger, more diversified company? 3. Do I have the inclination and ability to delegate decision making to my managers? 4. Do I have enough cash and borrowing power along with the inclination to risk everything to pursue rapid growth?					If the owner rises to the challenges of a growing company, both financially and managerially, it can become a big success. If not, it can usually be sold at a profit. Often the entrepreneur who founded the company and brought it to this stage is replaced either voluntarily or involuntarily by the company's investors or creditors.

Resource maturity	Greatest concerns: 1. Consolidation and control of financial gains brought on by rapid growth. 2. Retaining the advantages of small size, including flexibility of response and the entrepreneurial spirit.	Decentralized, adequately staffed, and experienced.	Extensive and well developed.	Expansion of the management force fast enough to eliminate the inefficiencies that growth can produce and professionalize the company by use of such tools as budgets, strategic planning, management by objective, and standard cost systems and do this without stifling its entrepreneurial qualities.	Quite separate both financially and operationally.

Appendix II: Creating a Global Marketing Plan

Global marketing has the same sort of relationship to single-country marketing as driving an automobile has to piloting an airplane. The actions are recognizably similar, but the fact that an aircraft goes up and down as well as forward radically increases the problems of control. The problems created by the global dimension demand an approach to the management of a business that is more structured than what might be needed or accepted in the home market. A back-of-an-envelope approach to market planning, sometimes possible in a familiar market, will virtually guarantee disaster in the global market. A detailed, written marketing plan and an associated budget are essential to structuring the activity, monitoring progress, and determining whether the effort is living up to expectations, should be changed, or should be terminated.

As with all plans, a global marketing plan has a number of well-defined components. These differ in a few key aspects from the components of a plan for the home market. Companies that are not in the habit of planning for their domestic marketing activities may have difficulty introducing this discipline with respect to their activities abroad, but the added risk and the scale of the required budgets should be a powerful incentive to start planning.

The main ingredients of a global marketing plan are:

- Global objectives
- Country targets and objectives
- Phasing of geographical development
- Method of market entry
- Product development and modifications
- Product sourcing plan
- Local marketing strategies

- Global organization
- Resourcing plan
- Timing

Your plan will be a blueprint for your company's global operations. It will cover all the issues that affect your ability to attract customers and hold them in the target markets. Thus it must expand beyond purely marketing topics, such as advertising and promotion, to include the logistics of supply.

Global Objectives

The first questions your plan must answer are:

- Do you really want to do this?
- Why do you want to do it, or, why do you think you can be successful?
- What do you expect to get out of it?

The starting point for the plan is a clear statement of your global objectives, which should include:

- Total global sales expected
- Rate at which global sales are expected to develop over time
- Proportion of total corporate sales planned to be derived from global markets
- Target break-even date on the global effort
- Total investment prior to break-even date
- Expected buildup in profits
- Proportion of profits that will come from global sales
- Number of territories that will be covered by the global plan
- Phasing in of the country marketing programs

Country Targets and Objectives

The global plan is an overall summary of intent. The real working content will be contained in the plans for individual countries. As Theodore Levitt pointed out in 1983, although standardized products can be offered to the global market, the marketing of them has to be adapted to suit local conditions.* This means that your global marketing plan must inevitably be a composite of the individual plans for each of the territories it covers. The country objectives should mirror the overall objectives, but with added dimensions, such as market-share objectives.

Phasing of Geographical Development

On the assumption that it is not feasible to enter all countries simultaneously, your plan should set out the order in which countries are going to be developed and the buildup of activity for each country. This is crucial. It provides the mechanism for ensuring that the overall marketing workload at any point in time does not exceed your capacity to carry it out.

Method of Market Entry

Your plan must establish the method of market entry to be adopted for each country. The same method does not have to be applied everywhere, unless one particular method is an essential part of your company's operational strategy. An organization that has developed by means of franchising, and has therefore built up a portfolio of franchising skills, is likely to want to deploy those skills in its global strategy.

The market-entry plan should include the following details for each country:

- Entry method
- Potential partners (acquisitions, joint venture, licensees), in order of attractiveness
  - Strengths and weaknesses of each potential partner
  - Basis for negotiations
  - Financial terms
  - Time scale for negotiations
  - Fallback positions
- Potential local agents
  - Territories or market segments to be covered by each agent

---

*Theodore Levitt, "The Globalization of Markets," *Harvard Business Review,* May–June 1983.

- Start-up
  - Locations of potential sites

Product Development and Modifications

If your product requires modifications to meet the requirements of global customers, the nature of the changes must be set out, along with their estimated cost, approximate time frame for implementation, and who will be responsible for overseeing them.

Product Sourcing Plan

The product sourcing plan states the origin of supplies for each country. Options are

- Export from existing plant in home country
  - Plant-extension requirements
- Export from a new plant to be established to service global markets
  - Locations to be considered
  - Plant size
  - Investment
- Buy-in from manufacturers located in the target countries or at some other suitable supply point
  - Sources to be considered
  - Strengths and weaknesses of alternative sources
  - Probable supply costs

In addition, this part of your global marketing plan should address the logistics of getting your product from the supply source to market.

Local Marketing Strategies

Segmentation

In all marketing, but especially in global marketing, it is risky and expensive to attempt to service all types of customers. For all businesses, some groups of customers are more attractive than others either because they are more likely to buy or because they are more profitable to service. The segmentation strategy identifies the particular groups of customers that your company plans to target and explains why those customers are of interest. Segmentation is usually based on some form of affinity between the company's products and the marketplace, such as geography (proximity to the source of supply or to major cities), customer type, income group, or activity.

For a segmentation strategy to work, the marketing messages must be targeted to each customer type, so you need to be able to approach the segments separately. In many overseas markets in which media and other channels of communication are not sophisticated, separate targeting may not be possible.

Pricing

The pricing plan for each country must take into account the cost of supplies and the prevailing competitive prices. Countries in which price premiums can be earned should be near the top of the priority list, although generally you will have eliminated from your list of target countries any in which it is not possible to obtain prices that will result in profits.

Physical Distribution

Physical distribution covers the logistics of supply within each country, including transportation methods and costs.

Promotion

Your promotional strategy will address the mix of promotional techniques to be used, the frequency of their use, their intensity, the objectives and target audiences of each technique, the cost of the promotion, and the allocation of responsibility for implementing each promotional campaign. The plan will detail:

- Advertising
  - Media (press, trade press, television, posters, cinema)
  - Agencies
  - Costs
- Sales promotions
  - Types
  - Sources of services
- Loyalty schemes
- Direct marketing

- Mail
- Telemarketing sales
- Sources of services
- Exhibitions
  - Specific exhibitions to be attended
  - Resourcing
  - Costs
- Selling
  - Size of sales force
  - Quality of sales force
  - Use of independent or contract sales forces

Global Organization

Having identified the many tasks that need to be carried out to market globally, you need to define the organization that will be required to implement these tasks. The plan for your global organization should cover:

- The central organization responsible for controlling and servicing your global marketing activities
- The regional organizations
- The local organization within each country

At its simplest, the organization may consist of an export department responsible for the management of export sales either directly or through agents and the shipment of products to export customers. As global marketing activity builds up, the organization will expand to include regional and local organizations responsible for the marketing activities within their territories and reporting to a central marketing department.

Resourcing Plan

The resourcing plan identifies the various types of resources that will be required to support your global marketing plan. It includes:

- Personnel resources
  - Numbers
  - Qualifications
  - Salary levels

- Financial resources
- Technologies
- External support
  - Sources
  - Costs

Timing

The timing plan puts the entire program into a series of time horizons that detail when each activity will take place and the date on which each activity is due to be completed.

Appendix III: Resources List/Contact Information

RESOURCES	CONTACT INFORMATION
Foreign Standards and Certification Systems	National Institute for Standards and Technology Administration Building A629 Gaithersburg, MD 20899 Phone: (301) 975-4040 USA
Breaking into the Trade Game: Step by Step Guide to Exporting	Small Business Administration in the United States Phone: (800) U ASK SBA or Consult your phone directory for a Small Business Administration office near you.
Basic Guide to Exporting: The Mechanics of Export Transactions	U.S. Department of Commerce's National Technical Information Service Phone: (703) 487-4650 USA Stock #: PB95-109799 or GPO Phone: (202) 512-1800 USA Fax: (202) 512-2250 Stock #: 003 009 00604-0

RESOURCES	CONTACT INFORMATION
New-to-Export Seminars and Additional Information	Commercial Service Internet site http://www.ita.doc.gov/uscs/domfld.html
Export Promotion Calendar Provides a listing of all D.O.C.-sponsored shows, missions, and Matchmakers	T.I.C. Trade Specialists Phone: (800) USA-TRADE
Export Yellow Pages Provides a listing of all manufacturers, service organizations, banks, and export trading companies that are involved in exporting	Consult your local phone directory for your local branch of the Department of Commerce. or Access the publication by Internet at http://export.uswest.com.

Notes

Introduction

1. David J. Wallace, "The Golden Thread," *World Trade Magazine*, October 1997, 18–19.

Chapter One

1. Marcy Burstiner, "Boiled or Broiled—A Fast Track Culinary Opportunity," *World Trade Magazine,* August 1997.
2. Eric Tiettrmeyer, "Even Better Than the Real Thing," *World Trade Magazine,* June 1997, 10.
3. David J. Wallace, "Sweeping Up Profits," *World Trade Magazine,* June 1997.
4. "Look Before You Leap," *World Trade Magazine,* August 1997, 13.
5. Ibid.
6. Ibid.

Chapter Two

1. R. E. Axtell, *The To's and Taboos of International Trade* (New York: Wiley, 1991), 24–27, 82–110.
2. R. H. Dodge, S. Fullerton, and J. E. Robbins, "Stage of the Organizational Life Cycle and Competition as Mediators of Problem Perception for Small Businesses," *Strategic Management Journal* 15, 1994, 121–134.
3. N. C. Churchill and V. L. Lewis, "The Five Stages of Small Business Growth," *Harvard Review,* May/June 1993, 30–40, 44, 48, 50.

Chapter Six

1. Steven Topik, "What Did They Know and When Did They Know It? The Growth of Knowledge and East-West Trade, 1500–1800," *World Trade Magazine,* October 1997, 78, 89.
2. Sam Quinones, "Making It Work South of the Border—Mexican Manufacturers Turn to Exports," *World Trade Magazine,* October 1997, 54–56.
3. Copyright Trade Point, USA, 1995, all rights reserved.
4. Ibid.
5. Dun & Bradstreet, Inc., 1996.
6. Quinones, "Making It Work."
7. James C. Shelley, "Export Factoring—Taking Advantage of Overseas Opportunities," *World Trade Magazine,* September 1997.
8. Ian Jones, "It's No Place Like Home—Europe Is Not Like the U.S. When It Comes to Franchising," *World Trade Magazine,* October 1997, 114–117.

Chapter Seven

1. Steve Barth, "Bridge over Troubled (Cultural) Water," *World Trade Magazine,* August 1997, 32–33.
2. Ruth Stanat, *Global Gold: Panning for Profits in Foreign Markets,* (New York: AMACOM, 1998).

Index

About the Authors

Ruth Stanat is the Founder and President of SIS International Research, headquartered in Fort Wayne, Indiana. Since 1984, SIS International has provided organizations with strategic planning, market research reports, and business development studies designed to help them expand into new markets. Formerly a Vice President of Strategic Planning for the Chase Manhattan Bank and a Senior Planning Officer of the Mars Corporation, she has held senior marketing and strategic planning positions with International Paper Company, Spring Mills, Inc., and United Airlines. Ms. Stanat is a charter member of the Society for Competitive Intelligence Professionals, a founding board member of the Global Business Development Alliance, and a member of the board of the Association for Global Strategic Information. Author of *The Intelligent Corporation* and *Global Gold*, she lectures around the world on issues of international business. She holds degrees from Ohio University and New York University and is conversant in French, German, and Arabic.

Chris West is Managing Director of Marketing Intelligence Services Ltd., which he founded in 1994. A graduate of the London School of Economics and fluent in French, he worked for the Supply and Planning Department of Shell International and for Eurofinance, a financial and economic consultancy in Paris. He returned to the United Kingdom to join Industrial Market Research, Ltd., a consultancy specializing in the analysis of industrial, commercial, and professional markets, and was named managing director in 1978. A member of the Market Research Society in the United Kingdom and of the Society for Competitive Intelligence Professionals, he is a regular speaker at conferences and seminars on marketing, market research, and competitive intelligence. He is a contributor to *Global Gold* and author of *Marketing Research*.

For more information on SIS International Research, please contact:

Ruth Stanat, President
SIS International Research
6219 Constitution Drive
Fort Wayne, IN 46804

phone: 219-432-2348
fax: 219-432-3031
e-mail: SISFWA@ctlnet.com
website: http://biz.ctlnet.com/sis

For more information on Marketing Intelligence Services, Ltd., please contact:

Chris West, Managing Director
Marketing Intelligence Services
109 Uxbridge Road
Ealing, London W5 5TL
United Kingdom
phone: 44-181-579 9400
fax: 44-181-566 4931
e-mail: chrisjwest@compuserve.com